the new investor's guide to making money in real estate
a strategist's handbook

the
new investor's guide to
making money in
real estate
a strategist's handbook
walter h. stern

GROSSET & DUNLAP
A FILMWAYS COMPANY
Publishers • New York

To my son, Roger

1978 Printing

Copyright © 1976 by Walter H. Stern
All rights reserved
Published simultaneously in Canada
Library of Congress catalog card number: 74–5626
ISBN 0–448–12468–8 (hardcover edition)
ISBN 0–448–11832–7 (paperback edition)

Printed in the United States of America

Contents

Foreword   7

Preface   9

PART I: THE LANGUAGE OF REAL ESTATE   13

PART II: REAL ESTATE FOR USE AS WELL AS INVESTMENT   27

Chapter 1: Your First Investment:
From a One- to Two-Family House   30

Chapter 2: One-Family House with Extra Land   38

Chapter 3: The Four-Family House   43

Chapter 4: Vacation Homes and Farms   48

Chapter 5: Resort Condominiums   58

Chapter 6: Stores and Offices   63

PART III: REAL ESTATE FOR ACTIVE INVESTMENT   73

Chapter 7: Land Investments.   75

Chapter 8: Home Sites on the Installment Plan   86

Chapter 9: Industrial and Commercial Buildings   90

Chapter 10: Leaseholds 101

Chapter 11: Operating an Income Property 111

Chapter 12: Operating an Office Building 136

PART IV: REAL ESTATE SECURITIES 143

Chapter 13: Second Mortgages 146

Chapter 14: Syndication 156

Chapter 15: Real Estate Investment Trusts 163

Chapter 16: Real Estate Stocks 169

Index 172

Foreword

When dealing with a subject so broad and full of vitality as real estate, it is unavoidable to resort to generalities. In this book, many variables are treated in light of current conditions, sometimes without allowance for future changes in these conditions. It is, perhaps, the only way to provide for eventualities—by not providing for them. For example, interest rates on mortgages fluctuate, and neither the rate of inflation nor property taxes will be the same ten years hence as they are now.

In providing financial profiles of properties as examples in these pages, it has been necessary to assume that there are no variables. Projecting the income to be derived from an investment, these examples are based upon the premise that, over the life of the property, interest rates will remain the same, rents charged the tenants will not vary, and that taxes and assessments will remain static. Even the rate of inflation has been projected without regard to the vagaries of the economy.

While this procedure is inevitable, lacking the power of prognostication, it is relatively simple for the reader to re-compute these examples on the basis of conditions that prevail at the time these examples are put to use. Since the basic principles remain, it requires only a mathematical exercise to re-compute the examples to factor in new economic conditions, such as changed interest rates, tax levels, or inflation. For ease of computation, we have used an inflation rate of 10 percent, even though it is no longer that high and may never reach that level again in the foreseeable future. Furthermore, sample rents given for residential or commercial space can only be approximate at best, since they vary even now from one locality to another.

In the same vein, these pages deal only in lay terms as they apply to legal and accounting considerations. As reiterated in many sections, the help and advice of legal counsel is a *sine qua non* of investing in real estate, and it remains only for the reader to have a general acquaintance with the terms and the legal concepts that stand behind them. Not only do laws vary from area to area, but many will be revised over the months and years during which this book will be generally useful. Consequently, generalizations cannot be avoided.

Finally, to make examples readily useful, descriptions of real estate transactions and property operations have been simplified; perhaps even oversimplified. Here, again, the objective is to draw a clear picture in broad strokes. No two properties require the same degree of maintenance, nor the same budget for heating. There are income, expense, and tax factors which have been dropped from these discussions entirely, lest they confuse the issue. Yet, if once the basic concepts are firmly seated in the prospective investor's mind, it will be easy for him to assimilate the detailed information which will flow to him when he actually becomes involved in the acquisition of real estate.

Preface

Some of America's largest fortunes were built through real estate. Thus, real estate is inevitably part of the thinking of anyone with the resources to contemplate building a fortune at all. But middle-income investors with modest funds are often discouraged by what they think the requirements of going into real estate are. The most forbidding being the quantity of money involved: everyone always seems to be talking in millions when real property is discussed. It also has an aura of complication: you just cannot close a real estate deal without a lawyer at your side. As an investment real estate lacks the liquidity of stocks and bonds which can be bought and sold over the telephone.

Set against all these are the reasons an astute investor of moderate means stands a better chance of success in sensible realty deals than he does in many other opportunities that come his way. First, consider that there is a finite supply of land from which all real estate emanates. To be sure, our vast country will always have millions of unused acres because there is no plausible use for them in our lifetime, but the limited supply of productive land operates as a positive factor. Second, the route between the investor's money and the property is shortened. Funds deposited in savings banks, for instance, are an indirect real estate investment, but the saver is not the most favored beneficiary. Finally, investment in real estate need not be a millionaire's vehicle, and that is what this book is all about.

I'm addressing myself to men and women who are the salaried employees, the skilled wage earners, the merchants, the neighborhood physicians or dentists (just about anybody whose continuing income is secure and whose liquid assets suffice to meet most normal emergencies, both personal and business-connected). We assume, therefore, that our investor has adequate life, health, and casualty insurance; maintains a savings account equal to at least a year's income at his accustomed standard of living; and has no debts other than the mortgage on his home. We also assume that he is inclined to consider other investments, for a number of valid reasons. One, to acquire some form of equity as a hedge against inflation which, I fear, will be with us for the indefinite future. Another, to enlarge his net worth at a quicker rate than can be accomplished by merely "stockpiling" his money, even at attractive interest rates. Still another is the challenge of the game itself, including its risks, bringing with it a bonus in newly acquired business acumen that eludes the prodigious saver.

For an objective look at the average man's or woman's role in the realty world, one must first discard the myths and irrelevancies. Luck is one of them. True, everyone has heard the tale of petty cash invested in some arid land that turned out to be two blocks in downtown Dallas. Another is perpetual motion, as I like to call it. This is the notion that vast fortunes in real estate literally self-generated themselves from a seed of pennies. There

10 *Preface*

were undoubtedly some interim stages, such as the infusion of major capital. And let us not forget that in every game where fortunes can be won, fortunes can also be lost.

The life of the middle-income real estate investor has no room for such fancies. The demand on his time by other day-to-day obligations is too great for him to take any but the most practical approach. His ability to carry risks is too limited for him to seek anything but a greedless appreciation of his equity. And, in this regard, he is perhaps luckier than the realty professional who cannot afford to treat his properties like a favorite house plant, which is fun to watch grow only if you don't stand there watching it.

Just how active or passive an investor in real estate you wish to be determines much of the course you should follow. If you relish the role of the active landlord, you may reap great satisfaction from operating a property on a day-to-day basis and do so quite profitably. At the other end of the spectrum lies the purchase of shares in a real estate corporation or investment trust, or becoming a partner in a syndicated real estate venture. Somewhere in between are various ways of owning real estate with a minimum of personal involvement, but not without detachment. The common denominator throughout these pages will be the availability of such investments to the nonprofessional with limited funds.

the
new investor's guide to
making money in
real estate

a strategist's handbook

PART I
THE LANGUAGE
OF REAL ESTATE

INTRODUCTION

Though real estate is not an occult science, it does seem to have a mysterious language all its own. Needless to say, the mystery disappears as soon as you become familiar with the language, which is really quite simple. So, for the reader who has had no previous dealings with real estate, a number of terms used in this book should be explained. Though they are all defined within the contexts where they are used, their meanings can be somewhat broader, so we offer them here first. The definitions are intentionally not technical, nor do they represent the entire scope of real estate language. They are solely to serve you in communicating with those you may encounter in planning and executing a realty investment. When it comes to translating contracts and other real estate documents, the advice of professionals and further study in technical literature is definitely suggested.

NOTE: All terms appear here in boldface type for easy cross-reference with terms when they appear again in the body of the book.

AD VALOREM TAXES Real estate taxes are levied by counties, cities, towns, villages, and school districts according to the value of each property subject to these taxes. *Ad valorem* is the Latin term meaning "according to value." Under a system of ad valorem real estate taxes, a house with a market value of $50,000 should ideally pay twice as much taxes as one valued at $25,000. This is not always so, however. The value of each property is determined by the assessor, who is a county, city, town, or village official. He and his staff, depending upon ability, manpower, and other variables, will re-appraise each property as often as practicable. Therefore, the value placed upon a newly built house may be closer to the real market value than that placed upon a house which has not been looked at, or reassessed, in three or four, or even ten years. Thus inequities occur. These discrepancies are even more pronounced when the assessments put on the same property by the county and city assessors differ substantially. Property owners have a right to protest these assessments if they feel that the valuation of their property is too high in relation to others. Protests are usually made to the assessor or board of assessors and, if denied, can be taken to court under what is known as a writ of *certiorari*.* If the assessment on a given house is then reduced, it may end up lower than that on an identical house next door whose owner chose not to protest. Ideally, the assessor, upon granting one protest, should make equivalent reductions on similar properties in the area, but this is not usually strictly observed.

Although many state laws require that properties be assessed at 100 percent of market value and make it illegal to assess them at more than that, many localities assess at far less, some even as low as 10 or 15 percent.

---

* Certiorari, from the Latin *certi*, to make sure, is an action in which you ask a higher court to review the decision of a lower authority to make sure an error has not been made.

The Language of Real Estate **15**

Again, what is important is that they be proportionately correct. If a community's assessment roll shows properties at 50 percent of their true value, a $24,000 house would be assessed at $12,000 and a $30,000 house at $15,000. The taxes their owners consequently pay would still be in the proper ratio. Usually, assessments at levels substantially below 100 percent occur when the tax rolls have not been brought up to date to reflect the increasing values (partly because of inflation) through the years.

AMORTIZATION   While the meaning of this term is basically stable, its application in real estate provides us with two distinct meanings. In the case of **mortgages** it is the term used for the gradual paying off of the loan. Translated from the Latin, it means the "dying off" of something. As you pay off a loan, you are bringing it closer to its eventual death. Some mortgages provide for amortization at a given rate each year, either to the point of paying it off altogether at the end of its term, or to a point where the remaining principal is considerably lower (see **balloon**).

The other meaning of amortization is similar to **depreciation** (see definition). It is usually applied to **leaseholds.** If an investor has control of a property under a lease for which he paid a sum of money, the amount he paid for the lease is amortized, in that a certain amount is set aside each year so that, when the lease expires, there is enough money in reserve to replace the depleted leasehold with another investment. Amortization of this type usually is deductible from the taxable income a property yields.

ASSESSMENT   As explained under ad valorem taxes, the process of assessment is the evaluation or appraisal of real estate in order to establish the share of taxes each piece of property is obligated to pay according to its value relative to other properties within the same taxing jurisdiction. The term assessment is also used to refer to the value placed upon a property, such as "the assessment on Harry Jones' house is $12,000."

BALLOON   Certain types of mortgages are structured so that only part of the total amount loaned is paid in the traditional series of gradual repayments (see **constant payment**). The remaining unpaid principal is commonly described as a balloon. It is due in a lump sum at the end of the schedule of payments, when the loan matures. Or, a new mortgage is taken out to cover *its* gradual repayment.

BUILDING CODE   This is loose terminology, but every city, town, or village has laws pertaining to the minimum requirements for construction. This body of law is often called the building code. Some of these laws concern safety in the construction and use of a building. Others deal with the amount of land which may be used, or limit the height of a building, though this latter group overlaps with **zoning** laws.

CAPITAL GAIN   This term is used in many areas of business investment. Essentially it denotes the gain or profit made when one sells something for more than one paid for it. Its importance lies in the fact that money earned as a capital gain is subject to a smaller tax than money earned in other ways, such as through salary or professional fees. For a capital gain to qualify for this lower income tax rate, it must be a "long-term" gain. According to

16 *The Language of Real Estate*

present laws, this means one must own the property for at least six months before selling it. Under present law, most capital gains of less than $50,000 are taxed at not more than 25 percent, depending on the size of the gain, as well as the size of the taxpayer's taxable income. It should also be borne in mind that the amount of the capital gain is the difference between what the asset sold for and its **cost base.** Remember, the cost base is not necessarily the amount the investor paid for the property.

CARRYING CHARGES   In its broadest sense, this is the amount required to continue ownership of a property year by year. Most people think of carrying charges as including taxes and the mortgage payments (which comprise interest and amortization, if any). Some purists prefer to confine the term only to the mortgage payments, while others take a broader view and include heat and maintenance as well.

CASH FLOW   This is an important concept in real estate, in that it describes not only the cash income a property brings but also so-called non-cash income. A $10,000 rental property will bring its owner, in addition to income from rents, $200 a year in depreciation. If he had bought a $10,000 truck instead of real estate, he would have had to set aside the depreciation in a special account in order to replace the truck when it finally wore out. In the case of the building, however, he had the use of the $200 each year, since, in fact, the building does not wear itself down to nothing. In planning an investment in real estate, it does make sense to include the non-cash items in financial projections, and this means dealing in cash flow figures. To cope in a practical sense with capital gains, cost base and cash flow, the investor is encouraged to work closely with his accountant.

COMMITMENT FEE   We will discuss situations in which it is advisable to shop for a mortgage prior to signing a contract to buy or build a building. In such an instance, a bank or other lending institution makes a firm commitment to provide the loan weeks or months before the money is actually needed. The funds must be set aside by the lender to be available when the mortgage is ready for the **take-out** (see definition). To hold this money in reserve, the lender charges a commitment fee. This fee is obviously less than the eventual interest on the mortgage, since the lender holds the money and can earn interest on it himself until it is needed for the mortgage.

CONDOMINIUM   This is described in chapter 5 in some detail. It is a form of property ownership in which each occupant of, say, an apartment building literally owns his apartment in the same way he would a private house. The owner of a condominium can arrange financing to suit his needs, paying as much or as little cash as he deems best and obtaining a mortgage for the remainder. The only differences between ownership of a condominium and ownership of an individual house stem from the fact that the condominium owner's property is physically within a larger property and, as a result, his ownership includes a proportionate share of the common areas and facilities, such as the public halls and gardens, the boiler and elevators.

The Language of Real Estate **17**

CONSTANT PAYMENT Most mortgages which require gradual repayment of the loan in addition to interest are structured on the basis of constant payments. In other words, the annual, quarterly, or monthly carrying charges remain constant—the same throughout the entire term of repayment. In a self-amortizing mortgage, the constant payments are calculated by the lender in such a way that, at maturity, the entire loan has been repaid. In commercial property, where the term is more frequently used, a constant payment consists of, say, 9 percent interest and 2 percent amortization, for a total of 11 percent per year. On a $10,000 mortgage, this means an annual payment of $1,100 a year. This will not pay off the mortgage when it comes due. If the loan matures in ten years, the amortization of 2 percent will result in a **balloon** of $8,000.

CONSTRUCTION LOAN This is a short-term loan given to someone who plans to erect a building. Until a building is finished, a mortgage cannot be put on it, since only a completed building can provide collateral for a mortgage. Consequently, a separate loan is needed during the construction period to pay for the work while it is in progress. A construction loan is usually given by lending institutions and financing companies only after they are satisfied that a commitment for a permanent mortgage exists. It is with the proceeds from that permanent mortgage, at the time of **take-out,** that the owner-builder repays the construction loan.

COOPERATIVE In one respect, cooperatives are similar to condominiums; they both represent varied ownership of apartments or other usable space within the same physical property. A cooperative, however, is a corporation in which the occupants own shares of stock in proportion to the size and attractiveness of their respective apartments. Stock ownership carries with it a proprietary lease which entitles the shareholder to occupy his apartment. In a cooperative, a single mortgage covers the entire property and taxes are assessed on the property as a whole. A cooperative occupant pays a proportionate share of interest and amortization on that mortgage as well as of the taxes on the property. In a condominium, each apartment is assessed separately and each occupant pays his own **ad valorem taxes.** In a cooperative, as in a condominium, monthly **carrying charges** include the cost and upkeep of common areas and appurtenances.

COST BASE A term used to establish, for tax purposes, the amount an investor is actually taking in capital gain from resale of a property. It is arrived at by taking the amount the investor paid for the property, say $10,000, and deducting from it whatever he has already recaptured in tax deductible income as depreciation, say $200 per year. If he sells the property after five years for $15,000, the capital gain would seem to be $5,000. But it isn't. According to the tax authorities, he has lowered his cost base of the property through depreciation by $1,000 ($200 per year for five years). Hence his capital gain is not $5,000 but $6,000, and is so taxed. The theory being that the $200 a year was untaxed as personal income because it was "set aside" by the owner against the property's eventual deterioration and replacement. However, it actually was income used by the owner since, in truth, the building did not deteriorate to the tune of $200 each year. As the

18 *The Language of Real Estate*

resale price shows, it actually increased in value even though it became older. Thus in resale, yesterday's tax deduction becomes today's taxable capital gain. However, the tax on a capital gain is still likely to be less than the tax on personal income.

DEED This is the most basic instrument in real estate. It is the document which conveys all rights in a property to its owner, subject, of course, to any restrictions which may be inherent in the deed or the property itself. There are several types of deeds, such as bargain-and-sale deed, warranty deed, and quit-claim deed. The differences lie in the representations made by the previous owners as to the extent of the salable interest in the property. A **bargain-and-sale deed,** the simplest form of deed, conveys property with all the rights and interests the seller has in it, but the seller provides nothing beyond that to insure that his rights are unchallengeable. A **warranty deed** assures the buyer that the property is unencumbered, and the risk remains with the seller. A **quit-claim deed,** usually used to pay off debts, merely conveys to the buyer whatever right or interest the seller may have in the property.

DEPRECIATION As alluded to in the definition of amortization, depreciation is the degree to which an asset deteriorates with time. In monetary terms, it is the amount of money which must be reserved in order to replace the asset when it is totally depleted. In real estate, of course, only a building and its equipment can be depreciated, since land has perpetual utility. However, as stated under **cost base,** a building need not lose value with age to the extent of its fiscal depreciation. The amount of depreciation an owner may write off against the value of his property depends upon government regulations which set forth the official life expectancies of various types of buildings. Here, again, it is best to consult with a lawyer.

EARNEST MONEY When buyer and seller of a piece of real estate have drawn up a contract of sale, it is customary for the buyer to give the seller a sum of money—possibly 10 percent of the purchase price—to show that his intentions to go through with the contract are serious. This is known as earnest money. If the buyer fails to go through with the purchase, he may be required to forfeit his deposit. If the seller, however, fails to live up to his end of the deal, the earnest money is normally returned to the buyer.

EASEMENT This is the right of an individual, company, or government agency to trespass on the property of another owner. Spelled out in the deed or supplementary document, an easement permits various uses of another's property, such as use of his driveway to reach a land-locked property or the right to construct a roadway, sewer, or electric conduit through the property. It could even be the right to conduct an annual ceremony on an owner's back lawn. Easements can be perpetual or have finite terms.

EQUITY This term denotes the actual interest of ownership somebody has in his property. If, for example, an owner has a $40,000 house with a $30,000 mortgage on it, his equity is $10,000. As he pays off his mortgage, he owes less and his equity increases.

The Language of Real Estate **19**

ESCALATION CLAUSE   Written into many types of commercial leases, an escalation clause provides that the rent a tenant pays increases automatically if certain of the landlord's expenses increase. Lacking such a clause, the owner of a building cannot charge more rent than the lease stipulates, even though he may be paying more in taxes, labor, or heating fuel than he did when he first rented the premises. Without an escalation clause he can increase rents only when leases expire and become renewable. Escalation clauses vary according to the costs to which they are tied. Some escalate only as taxes rise, others provide for many types of increasing costs. Most also require that the landlord prove, by showing documents to the tenant, how much the specified costs have risen. The amount of escalation allowed in relation to increased costs is also spelled out in an escalation clause.

ESCROW   A common business term, escrow refers to funds isolated as a reserve against an eventuality. In real estate this action is most often taken at the time title is conveyed. Rather than postpone the entire **title closing** because the seller has failed to provide something promised in the contract, both parties agree that sufficient money to fulfill the promise shall be held in escrow. For example, if the purchase contract provided that the seller repair or replace a faulty boiler and he has failed to do so at the time of title closing, sufficient money for a new boiler is held back from his payment and placed in escrow. When he subsequently delivers installation of a new boiler, the escrowed funds are released to him. If instead he refuses to replace the boiler, the new owner does so himself and pays for it out of the escrowed funds. Escrowed funds are usually held by a third party, such as the buyer's or seller's lawyer or the mortgage lender.

FEE   An esoteric realty term, fee is the basic right to ownership of land, or of land with a building on it. As in the case of deeds, there are several types of fees, such as *fee simple,* the most basic type of unencumbered ownership. Once again, it is a term best dealt with in a practical sense by a lawyer.

FORECLOSURE   When a motorist fails to make his timely payments on a car he bought on the installment plan, the dealer or bank can repossess the car. In real estate this repossession of a building, land, or both, is called foreclosure, and involves far more complex legal procedures. When a property is foreclosed, the lender who foreclosed it is free to sell it for as much as he can get. If the foreclosure sale brings more than what is owed the lender, he must return the overage to the owner whose property he foreclosed. Of course, the lender is under no obligation to sell the property at all. He can, if he wishes, keep it for use or as an investment.

FRONT FOOT   The size of real property is measured in many ways. An apartment is described in terms of the number of rooms it contains. A piece of land or a building is measured in terms of square feet. However, there are cases where the most important ingredient of size is the frontage on a shopping street or on a lake or ocean beach, cases in which the depth of the plot makes little difference in comparison. In such instances, the size of the property is described in terms of front feet for negotiating purposes, even for tax assessment.

20   *The Language of Real Estate*

GROSS RENTAL AREA   When leasing commercial or professional space in a building occupied by several tenants, somebody has to pay in some way for the areas used by everybody, such as the entrance lobby, halls, washrooms, even the basement. When a tenant leases an office containing, say, three thousand square feet, he must also pay for his proportionate share of the common space. That share may be an additional 150 square feet, and he will be charged rent on the basis of 3,150 square feet gross rental area.

GROUND RENT   When you own a **leasehold,** i.e., the right to operate a building standing on land owned by somebody else, you usually pay the land owner rent for the use of his land (in addition to having paid a flat sum for the use of the building). The amount of ground rent is stipulated in the leasehold when it is negotiated and may change periodically according to the agreement.

IMPROVEMENT   In real estate parlance, this is merely another word for a building erected on a piece of land. Thus, realty people speak of improved land, meaning land with a building on it, or they will speak of selling land with improvement, i.e., land and building. Occasionally, too, the use of the term denotes an alternative to raw land as opposed to improved land. In this usage it means that improved land already has roads and utility conduits on it, so it is ready for construction.

INTEREST   When you borrow money you are required to pay interest, i.e., you must pay money to a lender for your use of his money. The rate of interest depends on economic conditions. If money available for lending is scarce, the interest rate is high—it is more expensive to borrow money when it is in short supply. Conversely, when lendable funds are abundant, the interest rate is lower because lenders compete with each other to get their money out to work.

INSTITUTION   Mortgages are provided by many sources which earn income from lending money and collecting interest. The term institution indicates that the lender is a bank, insurance company, or pension fund, in short someone other than an individual or small business concern.

LEASEBACK   Fully described in chapter 9, a leaseback is an arrangement whereby an investor buys a property from its occupant and user and rents it back to him. The investor becomes the new landlord and the occupant becomes the tenant.

LANDLORD   This term derives from feudal days when lords, or the nobility, owned all of the land. Today it is a colloquialism for anyone who rents some kind of property to another person. Since, in such arrangements as **leaseholds,** there can be more than one "landlord" in its loosest meaning, it is better to use the proper technical terms **lessor** and **lessee.**

LEASEHOLD   Also defined more specifically in the book, a leasehold is the right to operate a property owned by another for a specified length of time. Under a leasehold, an investor may have the right to operate an office building as if it were his own during the term of the lease, paying **ground rent** to the landlord or owner for the privilege. He then becomes the

The Language of Real Estate **21**

landlord, so far as the tenants are concerned. When his lease and its renewal options expire, the building reverts to the hands of the land owner, also known as the fee owner. For this privilege, the owner of a leasehold pays a stipulated sum somewhat as if he were buying the building outright, though the amount is considerably lower. Because this ownership, or asset, is depleted when the leasehold expires, he must amortize the leasehold over the period he owns it, so he can replace it with another leasehold or other investment in the future.

LESSEE Anyone who rents a property *from* someone else. Tenant is a synonym. If you rent an apartment you are the lessee. In a major **leasehold,** you may be the lessee in that you rent the land from the land owner, but you are the **lessor** in that you rent out space in the building to others.

LESSOR If you rent property *to* someone else, you are the lessor.

LEVERAGE In the realm of physics, it describes a lever, which allows a person to lift a heavy weight with relatively little muscle power. In real estate, as in business generally, leverage permits an investor to obtain income from a high-cost property by using relatively little of his own money.

LIEN Basically a legal term, a lien is a legal claim by one against the property, or any other asset, for that matter, of another. The most common lien in real estate is a mortgage, which constitutes a claim by the lender against the property if the borrower does not meet the required payment conditions. There are also tax liens, nothing more than claims by the county, city, or village against the property if taxes are not paid when due.

LIMITED PARTNERSHIP This legal term is subject to slightly varying interpretations according to prevailing state laws, but essentially it is a form of partnership in which some or most partners have limited liability. Stockholders in corporations, for instance, have limited liability, meaning that if the company goes bankrupt, a stockholder, even though he's part owner, can lose only the actual cash he invested—his house, car, etc. are untouchable. But in a general partnership, if things go badly creditors can invade the personal property of every partner to satisfy their claims, should the assets of the partnership be insufficient. In a limited partnership, the limited partners are immune from such invasion, but there must be at least one general partner who accepts general liability and whose personal assets can be attached if need be.

MARKET VALUE For real estate purposes, the market value of a property is that amount of money for which a willing seller will sell it, a willing buyer will buy it, neither of them being under compulsion to buy or sell and both being aware of the best and highest use to which the property can be put.

MATURITY Used in connection with mortgages, it is the date by which the mortgage loan must be repaid. Normally a mortgage must be repaid at the precise time it matures. Some loan agreements provide that you must pay a penalty if you plan to repay it sooner. If, for example, you sell the property before the mortgage is due, or if you find a more favorable loan

22   *The Language of Real Estate*

before your mortgage matures, you may want to repay it. But if the lender is happy with the high interest he is receiving, and you wish to repay (actually prepay) at a time when he can't obtain such high interest in the market, he may charge you a penalty of a small fraction of the outstanding principal. Interestingly, when interest rates go very high, lenders will sometimes offer a premium to those who can prepay low-interest mortgages so that the lender can put his money out to work at a higher interest. All this, of course, must be provided for in the mortgage contract.

MORTGAGE   These are extensively discussed in the book. A mortgage is a loan in which a piece of real estate is put up as collateral. Actually, a mortgage consists of two parts. One is the mortgage note, which is the borrower's I.O.U. The other is the mortgage bond, the document which pledges the property as collateral in the event the terms of the loan are not met by the borrower. The borrower is known as the *mortgagor* and the lender is the *mortgagee*. Strictly speaking, the mortgage is given by the borrower to the lender, while the money is given by the lender to the borrower, thus mortgagor and mortgagee. In the vernacular, however, the borrower obtains a mortgage from the lender.

MORTGAGE ASSIGNMENT   If a mortgage is assignable, or has an assignment provision, it means that the borrower can transfer his debt to someone else, usually someone to whom he sells the property while the mortgage is still on it.

MORTGAGE COMMITMENT   As described under **commitment fee,** it is a promissory document in which a lender tells a future borrower that he will, under specified conditions, give him a mortgage loan at some specified future date. This date could be the completion of a new building or the time at which the prospective borrower is ready to take title to a property he is buying.

NET LEASE AND NET, NET LEASE   Used in commercial and industrial properties, a net lease provides that the tenant undertakes all of the general maintenance of the property he rents from the landlord. The landlord thus is not responsible for repairs, painting, utility bills, and the like. Under a net, net lease, which is a variation, the tenant even makes the mortgage payments and pays the property taxes. Under a net, net lease, therefore, the rent the tenant pays the landlord is entirely for the landlord to keep as his return from the property.

NET USABLE AREA   Under **gross rental area** it was explained that the tenant in a commercial or professional building must pay rent for his share of the common areas of the building in addition to the specific area he occupies. Leases can also be drawn on the basis of this latter space, the tenant's net usable area. This is the space which the tenant actually uses as his own. Contrary to the example given earlier, here a tenant using three thousand square feet pays only for the three thousand square feet. However, the amount of his rent per square foot will usually be higher to compensate for the fact that he is getting "free" use of the common areas, too.

The Language of Real Estate   **23**

OVER-RIDE   Business technique generally gives the organizer of a venture a chance to earn money from it without contributing money to it, or make money in excess of what his actual investment entitles him to earn. This is an over-ride, a free ride that sits over or above the distribution of the income from the venture when it is earned. In real estate, notably in syndication, such an over-ride is usually given to the syndicator who organized the group, selected and bought the property, and it is sometimes guaranteed to him before any income is distributed to the others.

PERCENTAGE CLAUSE   In a sense, this is a second cousin of the **escalation clause** in commercial leases. Percentage clauses are frequently used in store leases and enable the landlord to obtain a higher rent from his store tenant if business is good. In its most common form, a percentage clause provides that, in addition to the basic rent, the tenant pays in rent a percentage of any business he does above a specified volume. For example, a store tenant may pay a basic rent of $14,000 a year plus 5 percent of any sales volume his store may have above $80,000 a year. If he does only $75,000 of business in a given year, he pays only $14,000 base rent. If he does $85,000, he pays an additional $250. Through this device, a landlord can help a store tenant operate at somewhat lower rentals, hoping to share in the benefits if business is good, by the same token giving the tenant a break if, in another year, business is off.

PREPAYMENT PENALTY   Since mortgage lenders are happy when they have lent money at high interest rates, they are chagrined if someone pays off the mortgage in advance of its due date, especially if interest rates have come down. Indeed if the money market has softened, the holder of the mortgage may not be at all glad to have his money back because to keep it working he will have to lend it out at a lower interest rate. But lowered rates are precisely the temptation for the owner of a property to find a new, cheaper mortgage (at the lower interest) and use it to pay off the expensive old one. To protect himself, therefore, the mortgage lender may provide that the property owner will owe a penalty if he prepays his mortgage—all or in part. Of course, if the lender proposes to charge a prepayment penalty, or at least have the option of charging one, this must be included in the mortgage contract. On the other hand, if interest rates have risen substantially since the mortgage was made, the lender may be happy to receive prepayment so he can lend the money out at the higher rate of interest. In that case, he may elect not to charge the prepayment penalty.

PROSPECTUS   This is discussed in the text. It is a document which sets forth all of the details of a group investment. It is used in all types of businesses where investors are offered participations. Actually, the term prospectus should be used only for the offering statement as presented to the potential investor in layman's language. The more formal document, filed with the Securities and Exchange Commission or other regulatory body, is properly called a registration statement.

PURCHASE MONEY MORTGAGE   Fully discussed in the book, this is a mortgage, usually a **second mortgage**, made available by the seller of a

24 *The Language of Real Estate*

property to the buyer to reduce the amount of cash the buyer needs to invest up front.

REAL ESTATE By now this term should be amply clear, but nevertheless, it warrants a closer look. Everyone owns some sort of property or, more correctly, an estate. His clothes, furniture, and other basic possessions are known as personal property, as distinct from real property, which is land and the improvements on land. Real estate, or real property, is land and improvement.

REAL ESTATE BOARD—*See Realtor*

REALTOR Officially, only a real estate professional who is a member of the National Association of Realtors has the right to use this term to describe himself and his business on his business card, letterhead, and signage. More correctly, a Realtor is a member of the Real Estate Board in the community in which he lives or does business. Local Real Estate boards are affiliated with the NAR and, usually, with a state association of Realtors. Membership in these local boards is open to brokers, appraisers, mortgage brokers, and mortgage bankers among others. There are well over 100,000 brokers in the NAR.

Since it requires a code of high ethics, membership is a seal of industry approval which Realtors can display with pride. It can also give assurance to those who do business with realty professionals, but it should not be assumed for a single moment that a broker or other realty professional who chooses not to belong to the Real Estate Board may not be totally ethical and reliable. However, *only* members of the NAR may use the title Realtor, with a capital R, as it is a registered trademark.

REFINANCING This is merely a term for replacing one mortgage with another, at maturity or at any other time.

SECOND MORTGAGE This term receives ample treatment in chapters 9 and 13. Suffice it to say here that it is one of two loans made against a property and that, as the second mortgage, its claim against the property is subordinated to that of the first mortgage. A second mortgage, also sometimes described as the junior mortgage, may also be a **purchase-money mortgage.**

SELF-AMORTIZING MORTGAGE Used primarily to finance private homes, a self-amortizing mortgage is one in which the constant payments, be they monthly or quarterly, result in complete liquidation at maturity. The constant payments consist of interest and amortization in graduating proportions so that the principal is fully paid at maturity. While each payment is the same dollar amount as the preceding one (except sometimes the final one), the amount of interest is slightly less with each payment, and the repayment portion is slightly greater. It is somewhat akin to earning compound interest in a savings account, but in reverse.

SET-UP This is just a term for a brief summary of a property's financial operation provided by a seller or his broker to give a prospective purchaser a concise picture of the figures involved.

STANDING MORTGAGE Used occasionally for income-producing properties, sometimes also for houses, this is a mortgage in which the

The Language of Real Estate **25**

principal stands untouched and the property owner does not amortize it by gradual repayment. Instead, he makes constant payments of interest on the loan periodically and then repays the entire loan principal at maturity.

SYNDICATION   A venture in which a group of investors, known as a syndicate, is organized to buy and own a property. Syndications usually are, but need not be, partnerships.

TAKE-OUT   The transaction in which the property owner actually receives the mortgage money from the lender. The term is normally applied to cases in which a lending institution has committed itself to giving the property owner a mortgage, typically on new construction (see **construction loan**). The owner receives his take-out when the building is completed.

TAX LIENS   When a property owner is delinquent in paying his real estate taxes, the local taxing authority—the city or county or village —places a lien, or claim, against the property. It is, in effect, the first step toward foreclosure for tax default.

TAX RATE   This is a term often confused with assessment. It is actually the second half of the real estate tax structure. While assessment determines the proportionate share of local taxes each property must bear, the tax rate is the dollar amount levied against each dollar of assessed valuation. Let us say that a property is assessed at $50,000—its value for tax purposes is said to be $50,000—a tax rate of $12 per $100 means that this property is taxed at $6,000. In some areas this same tax rate is expressed as $120 per mil, meaning $120 for each $1,000 of assessed valuation. The result would be the same—a tax of $6,000.

TAX SHELTER   Certain cash income from real estate (as well as other types of business) is not immediately taxable or, to use another term, it is sheltered from taxes. Depreciation is one of these. Why?

If the building depreciates, or loses value, by $1,000 a year, the owner is not physically losing this $1,000 each year. Even though he deducts it as depreciation, he still receives it as part of the building's income. However, in theory he is merely receiving back part of his invested capital, but he is also reducing the cost base of the property by $1,000 each year. As a result, he is using the $1,000 each year without paying income tax on it. Yet he is not totally avoiding the tax but merely deferring it (see **cost base**). When he sells the building, all that untaxed depreciation he's been taking is regarded as part of his capital gain. As such, it becomes taxable, albeit at a much lower rate than he would have paid on the annual $1,000 in ordinary income taxes.

The tax shelter occurs in those instances in real estate where the depreciation of a building exceeds the income from it. As a result, the owner has no income tax at all to pay on his income from the building. In fact, the excess of depreciation over income from the building can be used to shelter other areas of the owner's income, such as part of his salary. Consider an apartment house with total rents of $50,000 a year. After expenses you have a net cash profit of $6,000, but the building is entitled to depreciation of $7,000 a year. You then have a tax loss of $1,000 a year with which you can

26 *The Language of Real Estate*

offset $1,000 worth of any other income you may have. In effect, the depreciation shelters some of your income from income tax. But as already stated, upon sale of the property, it will create an additional capital gain which is taxable.

TITLE As explained in the definitions of the **deed** and the **fee,** title is just another synonym for ownership, primarily used in real estate jargon. Having title to a property means owning the fee or having the deed in one's possession. Clear title means that there are no ifs, ands, or buts about owning the property. A defective title is one in which a lien encumbers the property or where there is a question or dispute concerning the owner's true right to hold title.

TITLE CLOSING This is the meeting at which title to a property is conveyed from one owner to another.

TORRENS SYSTEM The system maintained by some cities that keep a municipal record with title records of all properties absolutely current. It is therefore possible, without a title search, to determine almost immediately whether title to a given property is clear.

WRAP-AROUND MORTGAGE A second mortgage which is, in effect, wrapped around the first mortgage. This means that the holder (lender) of the second mortgage is responsible for interest and amortization payments on the first mortgage and collects from the borrower (owner of the property) enough to cover payments on the first mortgage and interest (and perhaps amortization) on the second mortgage. From the mortgagee's (lender's) point of view, the two loans are a single entity.

ZONING This broad term encompasses all of the legal and communal activities which help determine the character and future of a community. Local zoning laws are those which set forth the ways in which properties in various parts of town can be used, with a view to keeping the community viable and attractive. Not to be confused with building codes, zoning ordinances deal with the amount of his land an owner may improve with a building, the height of the building, the number of feet it must be set back from the road and from the rear and side boundaries of his property. Another set of zoning laws deals with the use to which a property can be put to avoid, for example, having a glue factory built amid a row of luxury homes. These laws usually also provide for so-called non-conforming uses. For instance, a zoning change prohibiting gasoline stations on a particular street will not force the operator of a gas station already on the block to close. Instead, it will permit him to continue operating it. Should he close it or sell it, however, it must cease to operate, in conformity with the now existing zoning ordinance. Certainly, no new gas station could be opened on that street. Zoning changes are usually described as up-zoning or down-zoning. Up-zoning means making the neighborhood requirements more restrictive, down-zoning makes them more liberal. Up-zoning may mean that population density may be reduced by requiring larger houses on larger lots, it may mean eliminating commercial or industrial activity from where it was formerly permitted, it may mean that office buildings must be smaller or have large plazas in front, or it may prohibit rooming houses or motels. Down-zoning does the opposite.

PART II

REAL ESTATE FOR USE AS WELL AS INVESTMENT

INTRODUCTION

At the root of everybody's involvement with real estate is the need for shelter. Short of camping outdoors, all of us make a basic investment in realty—the homes we live in. Be it private house, rental, cooperative apartment, or condominium unit, we invest a substantial portion of our incomes in shelter. Depending on the nature of our trade, business, or profession, the form of this investment varies. For those who must remain mobile for business reasons, renting a house or apartment may be preferable.

Geography also plays a role. There are areas throughout the United States, notably in rural and semi-rural communities, where rental housing is relatively unknown or unused; everybody seems to own his house. In urban centers, on the other hand, apartments, whether rented or owned, have become a way of life.

But whether it's a secluded cottage or four rooms in a steel-and-concrete beehive, we are making an investment. If you're the owner of a one-family house, this investment is quite visible. It begins with the cash down payment on the house. Your monthly payments on the mortgage include amortization which, in fact, is a piecemeal investment in the property toward the day when the house will be completely yours. In addition, you quickly become familiar with your investment obligations, such as real estate taxes, interest on your mortgage loan, and the cost of maintenance—everything from grass seed to replacing an aging boiler.

If you're an apartment tenant, especially a renter, as opposed to a co-op or condominium owner, you have the luxury of being isolated from the nuts and bolts of property ownership. Nevertheless, your monthly rent represents your proportionate share of the landlord's mortgage payments, of his real estate taxes and of the maintenance costs of his building. You are more aware of your investment if you own a cooperative or condominium apartment. You make a cash payment that launches you on the road to ownership and you are cast in the role of a property owner. While your subsequent monthly charges are akin to rent checks, you are kept aware of how your money is deployed to meet mortgage, tax, and maintenance costs, if only to help you itemize deductions on your income tax return. Your participation in the management of the cooperative or condominium can vary from a totally passive to a very active interest, depending on your preference.

The same is true if you're a self-employed businessman or professional. If you rent your store or office, your involvement in real estate is like the tenant's in an apartment. If you own the building, you assume obligations like the homeowner, and become investment-conscious. Finally, you could have the in-between role if you're in a commercial cooperative or condominium—a building jointly owned by its occupants for business purposes.

Now that we understand the principle that whether for living or business, whether owned or rented, paying for occupancy of sheltered space is a

Real Estate for Use as Well as Investment **29**

real estate investment, let's enumerate the reasons for owning one's residence at all.

Granted that in some areas, particularly the suburbs, privately owned houses are virtually the only living quarters available to the average family. But in those population centers where there is a real choice, and their numbers are constantly increasing, a family can weigh the advantages of ownership against the drawbacks. The balance quickly favors home ownership, and also makes the attractiveness of real estate investment immediately apparent.

First, the financial reasons. Once the down payment has been made, the "carrying charges" (mortgage payments plus maintenance costs) for a house are generally lower than the monthly checks you would pay for equivalent rental accommodations. Further, as we show later in detailed examples, costs such as real estate taxes and mortgage interest are deductible from your taxable income, thus further reducing the net amount you pay for your residence in a given year. The fact that you have shelter while gaining ownership is an undeniable economic advantage over rental accommodations.

To be sure, these financial advantages must be supported emotionally, for no amount of fiscal inducement can offset the preference of some people for the conveniences of tenant life. Confirmed renters argue that they like not having the responsibilities of ownership, including leaky faucets and shoveling snow from the driveway; most obvious is their outspoken reliance on the everpresent building superintendent and his mechanical skills to take care of such things.

Happily, to most homeowners, the security and confidence of owning their own homes is a distinct plus, beyond the financial advantages. They don't usually regard their responsibilities as burdensome. More often they take pride in the beauty of their lawns, trees, and shrubs, and despite occasional griping, relish the mechanical challenge of an occasional repair or even a major improvement or addition to their houses.

It should be clear then that purchasing real estate for use as well as investment makes excellent sense for anyone who has funds available to create added income, because you can get value from the investment by using it yourself, while it also increases in resale value. Probably the simplest form of this type of investment is the two-family house.

Chapter 1
Your First Investment: From a One- to a Two-Family House

Owning a two-family house probably requires the least of all special efforts normally associated with investing in real estate. Oddly enough, this investment results in a bit of reverse English. Only rarely does it provide the owner with direct extra income. What it really does is reduce his own housing outlays, sometimes even eliminating them altogether. Living for almost nothing, you can then apply these savings to a better way of life—a boat, vacations, or children's college educations.

The main investment difference between buying a two-family house and a one-family house is likely to be the sum of money involved. But with the availability of government-insured mortgages—through FHA or VA in the case of eligible ex-servicemen—the down payment for the former may be only slightly more than for the latter. Investment similarities are that payments for mortgage interest and amortization, taxes, and possibly insurance are made on a monthly schedule to the bank making the mortgage loan the same as for a one-family house. Maintenance is also much the same: the lawn, plumbing, painting, heating, and other costs differ little from those for a one-family house.

What then, are the differences? First, there is the neighborhood. Admittedly, the most posh sections of town are often zoned against two-family living, but this is not an investment for those who desire exclusivity above security.

Your First Investment: From a One- to a Two-Family House **31**

Next, there is the business of having a tenant. A serious business it is, since a tenant in a two-family house means fairly close contact, and the obligations of both parties should be squared away clearly in a lease that is as detailed as need be to insure compatibility on both sides. Tips on finding a tenant, handling and preparing a lease, and other important home-owner/landlord pointers are discussed later in this chapter.

Ultimately we are concerned here with the investment potential of a two-family house for those who would normally choose to live in a private house of their own. So now let's compare the economics of one-family and two-family houses as investments.

Bearing in mind all of the variables, such as size and location of the property, and age and condition of the house, to name a few, we should seek a middle ground. Anyone who is able to invest some of his funds in real estate is obviously able to purchase something more than a minimum dwelling. We will therefore zero in upon a one-family house with a price tag of $40,000; a house, incidentally, which does not have excessively large grounds or other atypical features. We will also assume that the house and purchaser are eligible for government-insured mortgage financing, commonly known as an "FHA mortgage," but that he will make a cash down payment somewhat larger than the permissible minimum, so while thirty-year mortgages are available under FHA programs, we will base this example upon a twenty-five-year term.

A $40,000 one-family house of this general description can easily be purchased with a down payment of 10 percent, or $4,000. This means the owner would obtain a mortgage of $36,000. Conservatively, he should figure on an interest rate of 9 percent under current market conditions. This, then, would be his monthly and annual budget for the major carrying charges:

ONE-FAMILY HOUSE

	PER MONTH	PER YEAR
Constant payment for interest and amortization on the mortgage	$302.12	$3,625.44*
Taxes (assuming middle-income, residential neighborhood)	150.00	1,800.00
Heat	65.00	780.00
Homeowners' insurance (fire, theft, etc.)	50.00	600.00
Maintenance (repairs by outside servicemen, painting, etc., tools, etc.)	100.00	1,200.00
Total carrying charges	$667.12	$8,005.44

*times twenty-five (years) is $90,636.

These are approximate figures. Taxes vary from one community to another. Heating costs could increase as fuel supplies dwindle, but we have assumed a plausible average for a well-insulated eight-room house. Insur-

32 *Real Estate for Use as Well as Investment*

ance rates, too, depend upon location, type of coverage, and other factors. As for the cost of maintaining a one-family house, there is the simple question of how much work the owner is willing and able to undertake. However, tools and supplies are always needed, and there are certain services for which it is usually better to call in skilled tradesmen.

To make the comparison valid, we must make certain concessions. Our one-family house has eight rooms. As a practical matter, the designs of most two-family houses usually do not provide for an eight-room owner's apartment. Seven rooms for the owner and four rooms for the tenant is the norm in post-World War II construction. The exception would be an older property originally built for, or later converted to, two-family living. In a comparable neighborhood to the one-family one, a two-family house might be purchased for $60,000, with a cash down payment of 10 percent, or $6,000. This means obtaining a mortgage of $54,000 for twenty-five years at an interest rate of 9 percent. The resultant budget would look something like this:

TWO-FAMILY HOUSE

	PER MONTH	PER YEAR
Constant payment on the mortgage	$453.17	$ 5,438.04
Taxes	200.00	2,400.00
Heat	100.00	1,200.00
Homeowners' insurance	70.00	840.00
Maintenance	150.00	1,800.00
Total carrying charges	$973.17	$11,678.04

ANTICIPATED INCOME

In a neighborhood such as this, a 4½ room apartment for a second family should bring a monthly rental of $325.00. You would do well in checking the rents charged in the neighborhood to determine this. Let's look at this apartment to ascertain the value. We are presupposing a unit containing a living room, dining area, two bedrooms, kitchen, and one bathroom, possibly even two. In effect, the tenant would be paying about $75 per room, not unusual these days. On an annual basis, the apartment would bring about $3,900.

Let us now look at the potential yield of such an investment. The difference between the down payment on the one-family house ($4,000) and the two-family house ($6,000) is $2,000. Assuming the owner is making the $4,000 down payment for his own home anyway, the $2,000 is the actual sum he is *investing for return*.

In carrying charges, he must spend $3,672.60 more per year for the two-family house ($11,678.04) than for the one-family ($8,005.44). But he receives annual rent of $3,900 for the apartment. When the $3,672.60 is

Your First Investment: From a One- to a Two-Family House **33**

subtracted, he has a year-end gain of $227.40 or slightly more than 11 percent on his $2,000 investment—a return which would whet any investor's appetite.

INCOME TAX DEDUCTIONS

But hold on, there's more. Remember that real estate taxes and interest on the mortgage are deductible for income tax purposes. First, there is $600 more in deductible real estate taxes on the two-family house than on the one-family. Second and more important is the tax benefit in deducting mortgage interest. Note that the first year's interest on the one-family house mortgage ($36,000 at 9 percent) it's about $3,200. On the $54,000 mortgage for the two-family house (at 9 percent) it's about $4,800. The additional $1,600 interest and $600 in real estate taxes mean that $2,200 more can be deducted from personal income if you have the two-family house. If the owner is in the 25 percent tax bracket, this would mean about $550 saving when he files his tax return, except that he must also pay tax of $56 (25 percent) on his $227 rental income. Still he has a net tax benefit of about $500 the first year. That's an additional 25 percent on his investment of $2,000. Not bad at all. It now seems clear that the one carrying most of the landlord's burden is, indeed, the tenant. The landlord puts up the $2,000, and puts up with the tenant.

FINDING AND SELECTING A TENANT

Depending upon local conditions, this is seldom a critical problem. Normally, an advertisement in the local paper will bring prospective tenants. For a commission, real estate brokers will be glad to help. In some cases, if you are buying a new two-family house from a developer, he will start you off with your first rent payer as part of the deal. Selecting the tenant and negotiating his lease may be another matter. Some people have an instinct for choosing a compatible co-inhabitant while others seem to learn the hard way. Undeniably, a two-family set-up, no matter how well a house is designed, tends to mean closer contact than, say, a four- or ten-family building. So care must be taken to select tenants whose personal habits and consideration for property and neighbors meet your standards.

THE LEASE

The matter of a lease is not to be taken lightly. True, renting out that spare room may be done on a verbal arrangement, but roomers are relatively easy to dislodge and usually are not long-term occupants. But as to tenants who are going to be sharing your house, it is clearly just as desirable to keep a good one for the long term as it is to get rid of a disappointing one, or at least to have the legal weapons to keep him in line while he is in the apartment. And this requires a lease. Aside from the value of insuring protection for

34 *Real Estate for Use as Well as Investment*

the homeowner-landlord, a lease is important in establishing the obligations of both parties, financially and in terms of services.

The simplest and most reliable way to get one is to obtain a standard local residential lease form, available in commercial stationery stores or from a friendly real estate broker. The forms set forth most of the provisions an owner would want in his lease and conform to the laws of the state and municipality in which the property is located. The lease form can be amended, of course, to suit individual requirements, but this might best be done with the help of a lawyer, particularly if there are conflicting points between the owner and his prospective tenant. Following are some provisions to which the homeowner-landlord should pay particular attention:

1. LENGTH OF THE LEASE AND CANCELLATION TERMS A two- or three-year lease is recommended. Ideally, this assures that the prospective tenant intends to remain in the apartment long enough to protect the landlord against the inconvenience and cost of re-renting the premises more often. However, if it seems likely that costs of such items as heating fuel are apt to rise substantially, it may make more sense to settle upon a one-year term. Under normal circumstances, the shorter the lease, the sooner you're able to raise the rent on the next one. More often, though, longevity of a good tenant may be worth more than a few extra dollars. The lease should also have provisions for cancellation. As landlord you should establish in writing your right to evict a tenant for nonpayment of rent or other infractions of your living arrangement.

2. AMOUNT AND METHOD OF RENT PAYMENT Once the monthly rent has been determined (see page 141), the lease should provide that the new tenant deposit two to three months' rent in advance. One month's is regarded as the first month's rent. The other one or two are "security payment," and kept aside in escrow. One month's worth protects the landlord against the tenant's "skipping out" some dark night, since the landlord has a full paid-up month during which to find a new occupant. Otherwise, this one-month rental is eventually applied as rent against the final month of the tenant's stay. If a third month's worth is obtained, it is held aside to cover any damage done by the tenant to the apartment. When he is preparing to move out, the landlord should a) inspect the apartment carefully, and b) if its condition shows more than normal wear and tear, withhold a sufficient amount to cover necessary repairs. What remains after unreasonable damage has been covered is then returned to the departing occupant.

3. RENEWALS AND ACCESS Printed form leases often provide for automatic renewal unless the tenant gives thirty days' notice that he intends to move out at the end of the first term. They also obligate

Your First Investment: From a One- to a Two-Family House **35**

the landlord to give the tenant thirty days' notice if *he* does not want to renew. You should check this provision carefully, in fairness to both parties. The important thing to remember is that you need time to find a new tenant if the lease is not renewed.

Some form leases specify that automatic renewal takes effect upon the existing conditions—same rent, same services. If you intend to raise the rent or make other adjustments in the agreement, again, it is your responsibility to notify the tenant of your plans thirty days in advance, to give him time to agree or find new lodgings. In any event, you are well advised to review the existing arrangement a couple of months before it expires to determine whether you want changes, particularly whether a rent increase is justifiable and obtainable based on conditions in your neighborhood.

The lease should also specify your right to show the apartment to prospective tenants if it is determined that the present one plans to move out. Not only should this access right be established in writing, but conditions under which the apartment is to be shown (advance notice for an appointment) should be nailed down in the lease before the situation ever arises.

4. SERVICES AND REPAIRS While houses are not all alike, printed forms are. In some parts of the country, two-family houses are designed to have the owner's premises downstairs and the tenant's upstairs. Elsewhere, a side-by-side arrangement with separate entrances is prevalent. Most two-family houses have a single heating unit, but some have two. If there is electric heating, and certainly where there is air conditioning, separate meters are usually provided for each family. It is important, therefore, that the lease set forth exactly whose responsibility it is to provide heat and maintain the equipment. Generally speaking, heat and domestic hot water are the landlord's responsibility, regardless of how they are generated mechanically.

There are many possible variations of how minor and major repairs are to be handled. Some landlords, especially those handy with tools, are prepared to take charge of all repairs, minor as well as major, and others prefer to get a high enough rental to compensate for the occasions when tradesmen have to be called in. Others find that it is simpler, and preferable to the tenant, to let the tenant worry about minor maintenance, such as replacing faucet washers, defective window shades and the like. If you choose this route, you should make certain that the lease permits you to inspect the apartment occasionally and to demand that certain minimum standards of maintenance be observed by the tennant.

5. PAINTING AND DECORATING The question of who paints the tenant's apartment, and how often, should also be settled in the lease. A paint job at move-in time and one every three years

36 *Real Estate for Use as Well as Investment*

thereafter is a standard provision. However, the lease should also clarify how exotic the tenant's decorations are allowed to be. If he has a penchant for dark brown walls, for example, it should be made clear that some of his security deposit may be withheld to pay the extra expense in covering his dark walls with light colors for the next occupant.

6. COMMON AREAS The use of so-called "common" areas of the property is another point to be specified in the lease. Is the tenant to use part of your garage for his car or for storage? Will you be charging him for it? What about some attic or basement storage at no extra cost? May his family use the garden along with yours? These and many similar questions should be answered before your name goes on the dotted line.

These are by no means all of the caveats a first-time landlord should consider. The purpose of citing some of the major considerations here is merely to alert the investor in a multi-family property to some of his legal responsibilities. There are also such matters as insurance, notably liability for the tenant's belongings and personal safety, which require consideration. Perhaps the best advice for first-timers is to consult a lawyer. The legal fee—for what is a routine matter for a lawyer—is small compared with the cost of a mistake. Remember, when you see a lawyer about a dispute for which there is no clear provision in the lease, it is no longer a routine legal matter, and the fee is considerably more than the charge for reviewing your lease in advance.

Now that you have learned how to get the near-perfect tenant, let us qualify this rosy outlook a little to keep our feet on the ground. Take it from the top and look at the potential variables:

1. In some areas of the country, the 4½ room apartment may not bring $325 a month. Taxes and insurance also vary in proportion to the purchase price of the property.

2. You must be prepared for the possibility of a vacancy, if you cannot replace a departing tenant right away. Against this, of course, we have assumed a generous heat and maintenance allowance which should cover a month's rent if need be, especially since there is slightly less maintenance with the tenant's apartment empty.

3. Since the mortgage interest per year diminishes as the loan is gradually paid off, the benefit from income tax deductions becomes smaller each year. Also, we can rightfully assume that the owner's income will increase, too, so that he may eventually find himself in a higher tax bracket. And, lest we forget, real estate taxes can be expected to increase while the interest deduction decreases—an offsetting factor.

Your First Investment: From a One- to a Two-Family House **37**

In short, from the first year's windfall, the net yield will begin to decline gradually. But the fact remains that the owner-investor has recaptured his original $2,000 investment in less than three years.

If he decides to sell the house, he can also benefit from the extra hedge he has created against inflation. Let us assume that he sells the property after ten years (the average life of a home mortgage, and therefore homeownership, is about eleven years). Let us hope inflation will be held to 10 percent a year. This means that, after ten years, the resale of the $40,000 one-family house should bring 100 percent more, or $80,000. The $60,000 two-family house would bring $120,000. Had the original $2,000 difference in down payments been deposited in a savings account or even invested in taxexempt municipal bonds at, say, 6 percent interest, its yield would have been no more than $1,200. Had the home buyer bought equity securities with the $2,000 difference in down payments, not even his friendly neighborhood stockbroker could have predicted what he would own at the end of ten years.

As we said at the beginning of our discussion of two-family houses, there is a bit of reverse English inherent in such an investment. Unlike most other investment forms, it does not produce tangible income during the period of ownership. Instead it reduces the owner's cost of living. In the example we have used, he ends the first year by spending nearly $700 *less* (after income taxes) than he would have if he lived in the one-family house. Considering all of the variables discussed earlier, he will continue to spend less of his cash as long as he owns a two-family residence, maintaining it well and keeping the apartment rented. In this sense, he has the option of enjoying the proceeds of his investment in various ways. He can take a more lavish vacation, save toward his children's college education, or invest the yield in other ways.

Chapter 2
One-Family House with Extra Land

While we are discussing the investment possibilities inherent in a family's primary residence, we should take a hard look at land itself. Land is the only finite commodity in the real estate market, and its value should be carefully examined. When we regard land as a finite commodity, we are aware, of course, that there are millions of acres in this country which are now vacant, will probably remain vacant forever, and for all practical purposes, are not a viable part of our land inventory. These are the deserts, badlands, swamps, and mountains which will never yield to urban development or agriculture. But within the accessible, usable sections of the United States, the supply of land is basically finite. Some land masses, such as the island of Manhattan, cannot be expanded. More isolated cities, it is true, can grow in many directions, but when they grow beyond convenient reach of the urban core they merely spawn new metropolitan centers and recharge that battery of land value. In effect, wherever we find a site for economic development, we lay our hands upon a part of the land inventory and give it an initial value from which future trading values emanate.

For purposes of this discussion, then, we can assume that any location in which an investor would wish to buy or build a home is one in which economic development has begun and sown the seed of established land values. This process dates back as far as the frontier towns where at least some value concept was attached to land. Meager as the income potential of these frontier settlements was, there was a living to be made there, which is why people settled there in the first place. Unquestionably, land was inexpensive and in ample supply, but even the pioneers of Laramie or Tucson *owned* the beginnings of an urban core.

SELECTING THE PROPERTY

Land as an investment in this context, then, could be an extra plot or even excess acreage adjacent to the family residence. Obviously, this imposes an added selection process on the home seeker. If you are buying a house directly from a developer, it is unlikely that you can acquire more than the basic plot allocated in his development scheme to the house you select. Finding a house for resale with an adjacent buildable plot is largely a matter of happy coincidence. But there are ways of going about it. The most modest way, perhaps, is to find a residential street which has not been fully developed and purchase enough land on it for two, three, or more houses and then build your own on the site of your choice. If you are somewhat more ambitious, financially speaking, you may consider something that qualifies as an estate in your area—a large house set in sufficient acreage that can be developed at a later date. This approach is not as forbidding financially as it may sound. So-called estates with so-called mansions tend to be a drug on the market nowadays, and they are often for sale at surprisingly low prices. They also provide you with a challenge in that, in addition to some initial repairs, they call for imaginative decorating and furnishing. If you buy one in an area where land values are rapidly increasing, by judicious and timely disposal of plots at the fringes of the property you can get back your big purchase price and have the big secluded house besides.

Regardless of how one goes about finding a suitable piece of land, or a house with vacant land, there are some precautions one should take. It is important, first, to know exactly what the local zoning laws provide. Is it feasible, under existing zoning, to build additional houses on the excess land? It may seem that way, sometimes, but there are such considerations as frontage requirements, rights of way, and other easements. Clearly, few communities would permit the building of second homes in backyards where the residents would have access to the street only by an easement through the front owner's property. If a street is partially developed, it is wise to find out why the remaining plots have not been improved with houses. There may be a reason, such as sewer capacity or other municipal restrictions, which could militate against your plans of selling the extra land for construction of a house. It is also advisable to learn the policies of the local planning or zoning board. What, for example, has been its policy regarding up-zoning by requiring that each house maintain a minimum of open land around it? Are its members considering down-zoning for stores or other commercial development—favorable to property values on your street but undesirable as a place to build a home?

THE ECONOMICS

Let us assume, however, that these doubts have been resolved and a suitable piece of land has been found on which a one-family house can be built. Or that you have found a house whose owner can resell it with an adjacent plot that permits construction of one or more additional homes. Then it is time to consider the economic principles which govern such an investment. In broadest terms, it is safe to say that the normal plot under a one-family house represents about one-fifth of the home's total value. This is a rule of thumb, of course, and rests upon the premise that the plot is of average size for one-family dwellings in that neighborhood. If this be true, it means that a $30,000 home property consists of $6,000 in land and a structure with a market value, or at least a replacement value of $25,000. On that basis, additional plots alongside the house should be worth approximately $6,000 each. Nobody would quarrel with a price of $36,000 for an equivalent house with a plot twice as large as the average. Even $42,000 is not outrageous when one contemplates the luxury of being surrounded by two vacant lots. Once we enter the realm of estates, whatever an estate might be by local definition, these ratios cease to exist. In some areas, a well-situated estate may command a premium precisely because it is an estate in the eyes of the owner and the community. Elsewhere, it could be a white elephant, a real estate monstrosity that could attract only a professional developer, and there may not be a ready market for so many houses, nor zoning for apartments, an industrial park, or a shopping center. In such cases, a once-lavish house can sometimes be purchased for the value of the land alone, leaving the buyer with a lifetime project of refurbishing and decorating.

To pin this discussion down to a viable example, let us zero in on a residential street on which three attractive lots are available, with a house standing or to be built upon one of them. Let us also assume that it is a street on which $30,000 one-family houses are the norm, indicating that each lot, of whatever is the average size, has a value of $6,000. The possibility exists, then, to acquire a $30,000 house with the two plots for a total of $42,000. This means that the investor is buying a home and, simultaneously, investing $12,000 in land for future appreciation. (With one extra plot, he would be investing $6,000.)

FINANCIAL LEVERAGE

By purchasing what, to all intents and purposes, is a $42,000 residence, the home buyer should have little trouble obtaining a mortgage of $37,000 under FHA, requiring him to make a down payment of only $5,000. Compare this with the alternative. If he were to buy a $30,000 home for himself and $12,000 of land for investment elsewhere, what would he pay down? On the $30,000 house he could obtain a mortgage of $27,000 and put down $3,000. On the vacant land for investment only he could, at best, find a 60

One-Family House with Extra Land **41**

percent loan, or $7,200, forcing him to pay $4,800 in cash. Buying a house and a separate $12,000 piece of investment land would cost him $7,800 in cold cash. It is not illogical, therefore, to consider the saving of $2,800 as the first form of return on investment. However, it should be set aside, at least mentally, to compensate for the future costs of carrying the investment to maturity.

MATURITY

This is the point at which the owner feels the land has attained maximum appreciation and is ready to be resold for construction of two additional houses. This is a good time to take cognizance of the emotional investment, too. We must assume that as long as the two extra plots remain vacant, the owner will maintain them as part of his garden, manicured for outdoor parties or rugged to serve as the neighborhood Superbowl. When the time comes to part with it, there may be more than a slight family upheaval over the prospects of trading a proud garden for a pair of new neighbors close by. There have been many cases, no doubt, when an owner has abandoned his plan to sell the land, feeling satisfied with his improved financial status to a degree which makes the profit no longer desirable.

But back to the verities of investing. Another source of leverage may be found in the real estate taxes levied against the house with excess plottage. Many communities choose to assess the entire property as a $42,000 residence. If the prevailing assessment practice calls for a 30 percent valuation, not an uncommon ratio, the property would be rated at $12,600 for taxes. At a tax rate of $10 per $100 assessed valuation, the yearly real estate tax on the property would be $1,260. If, on the other hand, the same owner purchased a $30,000 house and $12,000 land for investment, the local assessor might take a different view of the situation. He could readily apply the residential formula to the home property. This means assessing the house at $9,000, calling for an annual tax of $900. But on the land held for investment, his assessment might be at 50 percent of value, or $6,000. This requires taxes of $600. This makes a total of $1,500 a year. This is a relatively small saving, to be sure. If held for ten years, it provides a benefit of only $2,400, more than enough to pay the broker's commission once the land is ready for resale after ten years. It should be borne in mind in any discussion of assessment and real estate tax rates, that both are likely to rise. Properties are periodically reassessed to keep abreast of rising values (or inflation), and municipal budgets are constantly rising and thereby force the tax rate to go up as well. Still, there is a bit of leverage in buying land for investment as part of the family home.

THE MORTGAGE

Let us see what happens when the homeowner does finally decide ten years hence that the excess land is ready for sale. We should begin with the

42 *Real Estate for Use as Well as Investment*

assumption that general conditions have kept his street at least as desirable as it was when he moved there. Let us take into account, also, that his community has grown and demand for land has increased commensurately. Inflation at a rate of 10 percent a year, alone, should make his $12,000 extra land worth $24,000. Depending upon local growth conditions (in which direction has the town expanded? Is there commercial development on his street?) the additional land could well be worth $30,000. Let us settle for $25,000, however.

As we have seen, he invested $2,000 in the extra land, having obtained a mortgage of $37,000 on the entire $42,000 property as a residence. During his ten years of ownership he did pay at least $12,600 in taxes, probably nearer $16,000 because of tax increases. At least $1,000 a year of this is attributable to the house in which he lives. Only the remainder of $260 represents his investment, through real estate taxes, in the extra plottage. However, his carrying charges on the entire property were higher than they would have been, had he bought only the house. Let us see how:

A $27,000 mortgage at 9 percent for twenty-five years on the basic house would have cost him $226.59 a month, or $27,190.80 over ten years. The $37,000 loan, at the same rate and maturity, cost him $310.51 a month, or $37,261.20 over ten years. The mortgage burden of the two lots during ten years, therefore, represents an investment of $10,070.40. This amount, plus the $2,600 in added taxation and the initial $2,000, brings to $14,670.40 his total investment in extra land, purchased on a $12,000 price tag, which brought him $25,000 after ten years. This is a profit of $10,330. Put another way, the owner quintupled his $2,000 investment.

However, at this point the owner must refinance his original mortgage. Remember that the original mortgage of $37,000 was made against collateral consisting of the house and the three lots, including the two vacant ones. Now that you have sold the extra lots, the basic validity of the loan and its collateral has been impaired. In other words, the mortgage lender only gave a loan of this size because of the extra land included in the collateral.

Your property is now reduced to one house on a single plot. During the ten years of ownership, we have a right to assume that the value of the house and plot, originally $30,000 has increased to $60,000, reflecting nothing more than an inflation rate of 10 percent a year. Therefore, it should not be difficult to start over with a new first mortgage of at least $40,000. Its terms, of course, require that you immediately repay the remaining principal of the old $37,000 loan, which has been reduced to $30,000 or even less so the house begins the new mortgage free of previous debt. As a result, the refinancing will yield at least $10,000 cash to be used at your pleasure. You also have an option. If you have no immediate need for the extra cash generated, you may wish to make the new mortgage no larger than the remaining principal you are repaying on the old, thus reducing your monthly carrying charges on your house.

Chapter 3
The Four-Family House

Anything larger than a two-family residence becomes an actual income producer. In these pages, we will treat the four-family house as an investment for use, that is a home for the investor's family. Even though an investor might prefer to buy a multi-family building in which he does not live, handling the concept this way can lead us to the later subject of investment in large buildings. It is, perhaps, the best way to illustrate in simplest terms what real estate investing is all about. When we speak of a four-family house, therefore, we are using the term for demonstration purposes, for it makes just as much sense to consider a five- or six-family property, with one apartment occupied by the owner's family.

SELECTING THE PROPERTY

It has been a long time since four-family houses were built in most parts of the country. There are some such properties of recent vintage in California, for instance. In New York City, on the other hand, four- or five-family buildings are often the result of conversions of large town houses. It is easy to see, therefore, that the economics of such an investment have many variables. A converted town house in Manhattan is a far costlier property than a four-family house in a middle-income neighborhood on the outskirts of Los Angeles. With a little enterprise, of course, an investor could

44 *Real Estate for Use as Well as Investment*

build such a property in a community where there is a market for medium-priced apartments. He could do this and take advantage of his own design, thus providing his own family with as much living area as he desires, all on one floor or in duplex fashion. The remaining three apartments should then be sized to respond to the prevailing market demand, probably containing one or two bedrooms each.

Since we are concerned with the investment principles, there is no need to lock our discussion into a particular type of building. Rather, we should look at an average property of this sort and then project the results for some of the variations on the theme.

Let us postulate, then, the existence of a four-family residence which is for sale in an attractive middle-income residential neighborhood in, or suburban to, a fair-sized city. Let us also assume that the building is free-standing and surrounded by a small garden and, just for good measure, endow it with a four-car garage. As with the two-family example, let us think in terms of a location in a northern climate in order to include both heating and ground maintenance among the normal expenditures. The building example we'll use contains an owner's apartment of 6½ rooms, one tenant's apartment of 4½ rooms, and two of 3½ rooms.

Given these circumstances, a price of $100,000 should buy a four-family property. Now we must dissect the down payment and mortgage in light of the actual investment. Regardless of the availability of FHA or other government-guaranteed financing, the purchaser should put down more than the minimum in cash. Let us say he makes a down payment of $30,000 and obtains a twenty-five-year mortgage of $70,000 at 9 percent. The buyer should be aware that he would make a $5,000 down payment on a one-family house for himself (to get about seven rooms), so his investment in the *income* portion of the four-family house is $25,000. Using a rent scale of $75 per room per month, as we did in the example of the two-family house, let's look at the budget for this property, bearing in mind that this time we're assigning the owner "rent" on the same basis, since he would be paying for his shelter to some landlord, if not to himself. Once you become involved in real estate, or any business for that matter, as an entrepreneur, a valid analysis requires that you pay yourself for your own merchandise as does any customer. True, the grocer can take home a pound of apples now and then and scarcely notice the difference in a year's profits. But when, as in this case, you are buying more than one-third of your own merchandise, you had better put an equivalent amount in the till, or you will go broke —on paper at least.

On an annual basis, this would indicate a profit of $2,070 (income minus expenses). On an investment of $30,000, which is the full down payment, the primary return would be 6.9 percent. But if we consider that this owner would have made a $5,000 cash down payment for a one-family dwelling (admittedly more than the minimum FHA down payment) his real investment in the property for income purposes is only $25,000. Therefore, a more realistic primary return on his investment is about 8.3 percent. Yet, this should be examined a little more closely to perceive for the first time

CARRYING CHARGE FOR THE HOUSE

	EXPENSES	
	PER MONTH	PER YEAR
Constant payment for interest and amortization on the mortgage	$ 587.50	$ 7,050.00
Real estate taxes	250.00	3,000.00
Heat	90.00	1,080.00
Insurance	100.00	1,200.00
Maintenance	150.00	1,800.00
Total	$1,177.50	$14,130.00

	INCOME	
	PER MONTH	PER YEAR
Owner's 6½-room apartment	$ 487.50	$ 5,850.00
Tenant's 4½-room apartment	337.50	4,050.00
Tenant's 3½-room apartment	262.50	3,150.00
Tenant's 3½-room apartment	262.50	3,150.00
Total	$1,350.00	$16,200.00

the true romance of investing in real estate. It is the principle of leverage.

Remember that in the budget above, the owner pays himself rent of $487.50 a month. Of course, he can rent the 6½-room apartment to a tenant and find and pay for similar quarters for his own use. By being his own tenant, however, the owner receives the income tax advantages which would be denied to him as a tenant elsewhere.

It is in the interest and real estate taxes that he obtains his greatest leverage benefits, but there is leverage also in the other expense items, such as heating, insurance, and maintenance. Let us look at this more closely.

In the budget for a four-family house, we see annual real estate taxes of $3,000. Further, the interest portion of the first year's mortgage payments is about $6,500. This entitles the owner to deduct a total of $9,500 from his taxable income. Assuming him, once more, to be in the 25 percent tax bracket, he can save $2,375 on the year's income tax. Add this to the cash profit of $2,070 on the building, we now have a total of roughly $4,400. This is equivalent to a return of 14.7 percent on an investment of $30,000. On an adjusted investment of $25,000, as discussed earlier, this would be a return of 17.6 percent. How did this come about?

FINANCIAL LEVERAGE

Let's take a look at the definition of a lever, from which the financial term "leverage" is derived. A lever is a bar placed across a support, called a

46 *Real Estate for Use as Well as Investment*

fulcrum, much like a seesaw. However, the fulcrum is not in the middle, but more toward one end, thus creating one long and one short section. If a heavy weight—too heavy to lift with bare hands—is placed on the short section, it can be raised with little effort by pushing down on the long section of the lever.

In financial parlance, the same is true of leverage. In the four-family house (as in a two-family home to a lesser degree), the owner is receiving the income tax advantages of three families other than his own. And he is receiving it by investing only a little more money than he might invest in a house for his own family alone. Look at it another way. For a 6½-room family house, a $5,000 down payment would be ample. Therefore, the remaining $25,000 of down payment creates his leverage. How? By assigning two-thirds of deductible taxes and interest, or about $6,300 (of the $9,500 total), to the three apartments, he is creating about $1,500 of income tax savings for himself. On an investment of $25,000, this is a return of 6 percent from tax and interest leverage alone during the first year. Once again, we should caution that the interest part of the deduction decreases each year. But we can also project that an owner with the ability to invest is apt to increase his overall income and thereby move into a higher tax bracket, thus offsetting the difference to some extent.

There are other, less noticeable, ways in which the four-family house creates financial leverage for an investor. A comparison of the expenses in a one-family house with those of a four-family building also shows that other items, such as heat, insurance, and maintenance, do not increase threefold. As we examine other forms of real estate investment, the importance of leverage becomes increasingly obvious, but the owner-occupied four-family residence is a good way to make its acquaintance.

The important thing to bear in mind, upon examining the four-family concept, is that we have now entered that area of real estate investment in which the investor reaps actual cash income which he can use to improve his life-style or re-invest in real estate or securities.

It is only fair to point out the negatives of owning a four-family dwelling. It goes without saying that the operation of a building for four or more families requires more attention to maintenance than does a two-family house, if only to cope with the human foibles of three families of strangers. Also, housing trends change, and unlike one-family homes, four-family units may go out of style. Thus we have not dwelled upon the appreciation in value of such a property through the years, though the land alone is likely to increase in value due to inflation and thus provide a large measure of safety against a loss in resale. Then the vacancy factor must be considered since there are now three apartments which must remain fully rented for the building to be profitable. Still, the owner can live virtually rent-free if there is no more than one prolonged vacancy at a time.

DEPRECIATION

In examining the financial picture of a four-family house, we should not overlook the tax benefit of **depreciation.** In many states and municipalities,

The Four-Family House **47**

a building with three or more apartments is considered a multiple dwelling. Even if it is not, the owner has the right to deduct depreciation of at least those dwelling units not occupied by him from his taxable income. The concept of depreciation shows up more clearly in properties not occupied full time by the owner such as vacation homes and resort condominiums (see chapters 4 and 5).

As stated earlier, the financial example given for a four-family house is a composite of typical circumstances one might find in various parts of the United States. Prices and carrying charges can be considerably lower in, say, the outskirts of a secondary city. But so are the rents an apartment would command there. On the opposite side of the spectrum, on Manhattan's East Side or Philadelphia's Society Hill, for example, there are town houses that have been converted to four-family dwellings with price tags of $200,000 or more. To offset this, of course, apartments in such buildings are regarded as luxury residences and bring rents of well over $100 per room per month.

Chapter 4
Vacation Homes and Farms

All of us differ in our preferences for vacation fun. Some like travel, others enjoy a cozy hideaway in the mountains or at the seashore. For those who like to keep their options open, a second home for weekends and vacations may be ideal. Not only does it offer an attractive retreat, it could serve as a worthwhile investment as well. The owner can use it and, by judicious scheduling of vacations, rent it profitably at other times. Projecting the constantly increasing emphasis on leisure into the next decade, it is reasonable to assume that a vacation home can be resold to yield a handsome gain within a few years after purchase.

THE ECONOMICS

It should be pointed out that all costs connected with renting a vacation home—advertising, broker's commissions, and even the gasoline for the trips to show the house—can be deducted from the rental income before reporting it for income tax purposes. So can the cost of the furniture and its maintenance, if the home is owned primarily for investment.

There are really no yardsticks by which investment in a vacation home can be analyzed financially. The variety of properties, the types of locations in which they can be found, the degrees of maintenance they require, all defy generalization. Ideally, a refuge from daily cares has a personality of its own, and the seaside cottage or mountain lodge that is one's Shangri-La is apt to be a unique place, not a mass-production house. True, developers have discerned the trend and many are busily "creating" vacation communities. But from the investor's standpoint, they are a mixed blessing. If a newly developed vacation area acquires considerable renown, potential tenants can be counted on to flock there. On the other hand, the competition for such tenants is likely to be greater than it would be in more secluded areas. Moreover, the price of a recently built vacation home can rival that of a primary residence in or near the city, and the house would have to command substantial season rentals to become viable as a true investment.

We must distinguish between various objectives of investing in a second home. Probably the most common approach is to look upon the property as essentially a family center during weekends and vacations. The only reason to seek rental income is to offset all or part of the cost of owning the property. This is necessary to those whose incomes would not otherwise support a second residence. It also makes sense for families not committed to spending every vacation there, since the vacation home can be rented for entire seasons in years the owners prefer to travel. In any case, the house remains a second home for the family—it is rented only to get the contribution required for its own upkeep or when the owner has no need for it.

At the opposite end of the spectrum is the investor, whose basic interest is in the income and capital gain potential of the property. Rentability is the primary consideration, and he uses the vacation home, if at all, only when it cannot be profitably rented, i.e., in the off seasons. His vacation budget goes for travel or resorts and is not contingent upon any income from the second home. By the same token, the home is itself economically self-sufficient.

VACATION HOMES AS INVESTMENTS

When we speak of buying vacation homes, many of the rules of thumb pertaining to a year-round residence fall by the wayside. For example, the land under an urban or suburban house normally represents one-fifth the property's total value. Not so in the country. A cottage in the mountains may be set amid acres of woodlands worth far more than the small, and possibly aging structure itself. At the seashore, the plot may be small but, by virtue of its water frontage, represents the bulk of the property's cost. Then there are farms, producing agricultural income above and beyond the rental revenue of the main house.

Maintenance costs also vary from the urban and suburban norm. Heating, for example, becomes a negligible factor in many cases. Even insurance can be substantially less than in the city, especially if the house is small. Real estate taxes in rural hamlets are generally amazingly low, due to the modest financial requirements of school systems and the paucity of municipal services.

50 *Real Estate for Use as Well as Investment*

On the other side of the coin, we must consider the cost and maintenance of furnishings. Not only must a rental vacation home be furnished and equipped attractively by the owner, but replacements are more frequent. Tenants of furnished premises are known for their propensity to stain carpets and upholstery or park iced drinks on polished wood.

THE MORTGAGE

These, too, differ for vacation homes. Mortgage lenders must reckon with the fact that the purchaser may already be paying off a loan on his primary residence. In this regard, the apartment renter is more fortunate, since his only mortgage is the one on the vacation house. An investor who does own his house in the city or suburbs should be prepared to make a down payment of at least 25 percent of the price of his vacation house, even more when the bulk of the value represents land.

FINDING A TENANT

Finding a tenant for a vacation house requires a somewhat different strategy than it does in urban areas because urban areas tend to produce a natural demand for apartments. But when it comes to season rentals, away from the city, the market is far more diffused. Prospects from far-ranging areas are sometimes less determined to find rental accommodations, since there are motels and other options open to them. And the renting season, summer or winter, is relatively short.

First, it should be determined whether the house to be rented is in an acknowledged vacation area. In known summer or winter (skiing) resort areas there is a built-in clientele which comes to scout the locale seasonally. They visit the local brokers, search for "For Rent" signs and even visit merchants to glean information about rentals. You can place your house with local brokers or find your own tenant by advertising, the same as you did in the city or suburbs.

But the house in a secluded spot calls for a different strategy. Here, real estate brokers in the nearest population center can be very productive. They have a list of past clients and future prospects who can be contacted. Meanwhile do not overlook the power of advertising. When and where?

Again start early—well before the summer or winter season. People make vacation plans far in advance. Three months before the date of occupancy is not too soon. The most obvious medium is the classified advertising section of your local newspaper, if you live in or near a sizable city. But remember that a classified ad will be seen only by those who deliberately scan the listings of vacation houses in search of such a place. Others are ambivalent about renting a house for the summer or winter, and they must be enticed. So consider the business page of the paper or even the *Wall Street Journal* for attracting the breadwinners nurturing the most idyllic dreams of retreat from reality. You can also attract prospects—and perhaps at less cost—through more specialized media. Many labor unions publish weekly or monthly newspapers. Physicians read medical journals. There are trade publications for plumbers, electricians, and just about every industry imaginable. Many of these are monthlies or quarterlies, and you must be certain not to miss their deadlines. If you are lucky enough to have a friend in the advertising business, take him to lunch and ask him to guide you. If not, go to your local library and become acquainted with the N. W. Ayer *Directory of Publications*. It will give you advertising rates, deadlines, and most other information you will need.

FURNISHING AND RENTING THE HOUSE

As to furnishings, the house should be furnished, carpeted, and equipped in much the same way as the owner would want it to be for his own use. There are those who have a special liking for "roughing it" with primitive, camplike accommodations, but this will not do if you wish to attract the broadest possible cross section of potential tenants. At the beach, or even in the mountains, carpeting may not be desirable, but curtains always are. Plastic tableware is utilitarian, but china, however inexpensive, shows you care. Stainless steel utensils are fine—sterling is unnecessary in the country. Are you accustomed to a dishwasher, clothes washer, and dryer? Then assume your tenant is, too. Television, radio, alarm clock, garden furniture, and gardening tools should be part of the deal. If the property has a dock and you own a small boat, with or without motor, take advantage of the tax write-off (depreciation on equipment) and make it available to the tenant by adjusting your rental accordingly. And be sure the dock is in good and safe repair. Use of your favorite fishing rod or golf clubs is an optional matter, something you can best judge when you meet your tenant.

The business of renting a vacation home is more cumbersome than renting an apartment in your year-round house simply because, to show prospects your property, you must travel back and forth to your Shangri-La. But, you can arrange several appointments on a weekend and enjoy the change of scene too, so this gives the trip a dual purpose. Besides, a lived-in residence has a warmer appearance, provided it is kept tidy, and thus becomes easier to rent. As an alternative, you can probably make arrangements with a nearby broker to show the house for a partial commission.

You also have the right to set some ground rules. No fingerpainting on the wallpaper, for instance. Children are hard to rule out, but pets are not, if you have a true aversion to them. As a favor to your tenant as well as to yourself, it behooves you to alert him to any unusual kinks in the equipment, such as a balky garage door. It averts damage or, at least, the resulting recriminations. Best of all, protect both parties with a lease, which sets forth precisely what the terms for the season's arrangement are, the same as in renting a year-round apartment in your house. Forms for vacation-home leases are readily available in commercial stationery stores. If you are dealing with a real estate broker, he will be glad to draw one up for you.

ANTICIPATED INCOME

Now, to find your leisure-time haven and see how you can enjoy it and derive profit from it too. The investor (and his family) must decide where it should be located, whether shore or hills, be it rustic or modern. But keep in mind, if it is too inaccessible, it will be difficult to rent. Location is a personal choice, but less personal is the amount of money spent. If you were buying a house merely for family vacations, the investment would be dictated entirely by what the budget allows. But since income and profit are the objectives here, two factors come into play. Even if the funds for such an investment are substantial, there is the question of how much rental from tenants would be required to make it pay off. The more luxurious the vacation house, the narrower the range of tenants capable of renting it. There is a limit on how much money should be invested in a second home for profit unless, of course, one is fortunate enough to find an attractive site with more than one cottage on it. But let us restrict ourselves to the one-house property concept for these illustrations.

THE BUDGET

Take, for example, a $20,000 property of which the value of the land represents $10,000 and the house itself the other $10,000. From an investment point of view, it would be wise to invest $10,000 cash and obtain a twenty-five-year mortgage for the balance at 9 percent interest. The annual budget would look something like this:

Interest and amortization on the mortgage	$1,007.04
Real estate taxes	200.00
Utilities (heat, gas, electric) assuming seasonal use	90.00
Insurance (including furnishings but not assuming such extras as boats)	400.00
General maintenance (assuming seasonal use)	300.00
Total	$1,997.04

Rental income from such a property would vary. Certainly, a one-month tenant would pay the most, probably $1,000. A tenant who commits himself for an entire three-month season deserves a break, and might pay only $2,500, or even as little as $2,000. But many vacation homes lend themselves to short-term rentals, such as Christmas or Easter weeks. So let us take the mean of $2,500 annual rental income. From this we deduct the $1,997 it costs to maintain the property each year, leaving us with a net cash profit of $503 or 5 percent.

Notice that in the case of the vacation home, for the first time, we will *not* compute the income tax deductibility of real estate taxes and interest on the mortgage. Instead, we have already taken *all* of the costs of operating

Vacation Homes and Farms **53**

our investment, including the taxes and interest, and subtracted them, like any business expense, from gross rental income to arrive at a net income of $503.

This is a good time to look at an important concept of real estate investing—**cash flow.** Simply defined, cash flow is the sum of all income, both cash and noncash, which a property generates. The most important ingredient of cash flow is **depreciation** and this is also a good time to get a clear picture of how it works in real estate.

Depreciation is the name given to money put aside for the eventual replacement of income-producing assets, such as machinery, equipment, or store fixtures. The owner of a $6,000 delivery truck sets aside $1,500 depreciation each year so that, four years hence when the truck breaks down completely, he will have the $6,000 to buy a new one. Since the truck is required to produce income, the $1,500 depreciation is regarded as a business expense and subtracted from the income derived from the truck's operation. The theory being that the owner has to set aside such replacement money—and cannot spend it as part of his real income—lest he face the problem of buying a new truck without sufficient funds and going out of business.

Real estate is different. The owner of an income-producing property also sets aside depreciation, or replacement money, against the day when the building becomes useless. But he does this on paper only, because a properly built structure not only has almost endless utility, but its monetary value may be greater in the future than when it was bought. So the depreciation set aside can be regarded as usable income or, more properly, as cash flow. Remember, *only the value of the structure can be depreciated,* since land does not wear out, and this can be done for income tax purposes only if the property serves as an investment for income.

TAX DEDUCTIBILITY

Now let us see how this works with our example. The real, or cash, income from the property is $502.96. Let's say the home, assuming it is not new, might be regarded by the Internal Revenue Service to have a remaining useful life of twenty-five years. Annual depreciation of a $10,000 house at 4 percent means $400 a year. Since this money need not actually be set aside, it is added to the $502.96, for a total of $902.96. The cash flow in our example, therefore, is about 9 percent a year on the cash investment of $10,000.

Now we see that the $400 depreciation may also be deducted as an expense, so we wind up paying taxes on only $102.96 of income. You should also note that additional business expenses can include the cost of advertising the house, travel to show it to prospective tenants, and possibly a commission to a real estate broker.

Admittedly, a return of 9 percent on an investment such as this will not

54 *Real Estate for Use as Well as Investment*

set the world on fire.* Alternatively, it will be lessened if the owner rents for a shorter period, preferring to use the house himself most of the time. If so, he should at least mentally calculate the value of his own usage. If, however, the owner uses the house more than half of the time, his right to take depreciation and treat it as an investment may be in question.

But the real attractiveness of investing in a vacation home is that it provides a hedge against inflation through eventual resale. Let's assume the house is sold after ten years. Though of course it is difficult to estimate the sale price, inflation alone, at 10 percent a year, should raise the value to $40,000. Since this is the most conservative guess, let us pursue its implications.

There is a net gain of $20,000 before capital gains taxes. However, so far as taxes are concerned, the gain is actually greater because of the depreciation we have taken over those ten years. We have written off $400 depreciation a year, or a total of $4,000. The cost base of the house then has been reduced by $4,000 to $16,000. In the eyes of the Internal Revenue Service, the gain on the resale of the property is not $20,000, but $24,000. Taxable at the capital gains rate of 25 percent, or $6,000, the after-tax profit is $18,000. But let us not forget through the same ten years, the mortgage has been paid down to about $8,000. The net result to the investor, therefore, takes on the following dimensions:

He receives a check from the purchaser of	$40,000
He next pays the mortgage lender the balance of the principal of his mortgage, about	8,000
This leaves him with cash of	$32,000
He next pays capital gains tax of	6,000
This leaves him with a net cash profit of	$26,000

Considering his original cash investment of $10,000, he has made a profit of $16,000, or 160 percent. Pro-rated over the ten years he held the property, it means an additional 16 percent and, in retrospect, gave him a total yield of 24.5 percent a year.

In these illustrations we have omitted some of the incidental costs of buying and selling property, such as title search, title insurance, and other closing costs, such as lawyers' fees. Unquestionably, they affect the final results to some degree, but we must deal in approximations. This is true also of taxes, insurance premiums, and indeed, of the very essence of any example, including purchase and sales price as well as rentals.

Needless to say, vacation houses come in all sizes and vintages. A shortage of gasoline can make a home-away-from-home undesirable altogether. At the same time, increased airline fares and resort hotel prices can refresh the appeal of a summer in the nearby countryside. The popular-

*There are variables, as we said, which could make the return greater or lesser. Some homes can be rented for more than a three-month season and thus bring in more income.

Vacation Homes and Farms **55**

ity of any vacation area varies with fashions. Witness the current ascendancy of skiing. There is a built-in unpredictability in all real estate ventures, though far less, perhaps, than one finds in the securities market. In the case of the vacation home, one thing is predictable. When the demand slackens, it is always available for the owner's enjoyment, at virtually no cost, until the day it is sold at a profit.

VACATION FARMS

One variation on this theme is a vacation farm, which appeals to those who would like to be farmers without becoming enmeshed in the day-to-day work of agriculture. Their "farming" gives each sojourn in the country a meaningful purpose. We are talking here about real farms that, to be viable investments, must be worked and require the presence of a full-time farmer. Often he is the seller and will stay on to manage the farm as a tenant. Otherwise a tenant must be found to work the property. Properties available for such investment can be small dairy, poultry, and truck farms; cattle ranches, with the acreage they require, are usually beyond the means of the middle-income investor. In some areas, properties of this type can be found through special brokers. Farms are also occasionally advertised in the newspapers of nearby cities.

SELECTING A VACATION FARM

Without examining the details too closely, since they vary widely, let us consider the basic principles and the physical requisites of an investment farm.

First its acreage should be sufficient to support the type of agriculture in which it is engaged, a standard which you can determine from neighboring farms or, better yet, from literature available from the U. S. Department of Agriculture. The farm should be at least self-supporting. If it were really profitable, it probably would not have been offered for sale in the first place.

Second, since even a small farm must be worked to be a viable investment, a tenant-farmer must be found and paid. There are several arrangements to cover this. One is to pay him an outright salary for his work, which should include caretaking and maintenance of the main house. Under this concept, the agricultural profits accrue to the owner-investor. If the farmer is *not* salaried, he keeps the earnings from the soil and livestock but pays a reasonable rental for his living quarters. There are many possible compromises between these two arrangements. Regardless of the terms, however, the investor assumes the role of the farmer in the eyes of the authorities. This takes on special meaning when we consider the many benefits the government provides the agricultural industry. There are price supports for certain crops and subsidies for others. There is a depletion allowance for many types of livestock, which is essentially an accelerated

56 *Real Estate for Use as Well as Investment*

form of depreciation. How these benefits are applied depends, of course, upon the particular arrangement with the tenant farmer. Of obvious importance is the question of who pays for the livestock. Similar consideration must be given to whose responsibility it is to pay for fodder, seed, mechanical equipment and its maintenance. In the case of the gentleman farmer, the investor, these costs usually become his responsibility under any plan whereby the working farmer is salaried.

Third, it should have at least two residences—one to serve as the owner's vacation residence and the other to be the tenant farmer's year-round quarters. A farmhouse large enough to accommodate both families may serve the purpose, but it imposes obvious inconveniences. It certainly is less likely to attract summer residents when the owner wants to rent to vacationers. At best, a single main house might be an interim solution for the investor planning to build a new residence at a later date.

THE ECONOMICS

Since our concern is real estate, we would normally focus on the profitability of the house, not the agriculture, but in this type of investment the two are merged beyond distinction. As a general rule, mortgages on farms are less generous than those on ordinary houses. The down payment may range as high as 50 percent of the price, particularly if the purchase includes substantial livestock and equipment. Much of the cost must be assigned against the forthcoming income from the farming operation. The main house—the crux of the whole investment from our point of view —should be viewed as a "steal."

What do we mean by this? Let us say that anywhere else, the farmhouse standing by itself on a few acres should be worth $25,000. On a farm, by the time all possible factors of the cost have been allocated to the agricultural side of the enterprise, the remaining cost, which is assigned to the main house, might be as little as $10,000. The same is true of carrying charges. Bear in mind that the farmer maintains the building. Real estate taxes on the property can be allocated, in large part, to the farming operation, as can insurance and maintenance, especially since the farmer will take care of routine repairs.

ANTICIPATED INCOME

In view of these cost allocations, income from summer rental of the main house can be almost a total profit. As for the allocations themselves, the investor will quickly learn to use good judgment. If the farming operation is reasonably successful, he can ascribe more of his carrying costs to them and proportionately less to the farmhouse. If farming results are marginal, he becomes more dependent upon the yield of his summer rentals in order to compensate for the increased carrying charges ascribed to the main building.

Vacation Homes and Farms **57**

The eventual profit of a resale, of course, is contingent upon the profitability of the agricultural operation. The acreage has increasing value, to be sure, but the main house is basically an adjunct to the farm as a whole, and it is extremely hazardous to project profits on resale on this basis.

There is no gainsaying the fact that this is an investment suitable only to those who possess either knowledge of, or the willingness to learn, the agricultural business. Included in this understanding must be considerable insight into bank borrowing for non-real estate purposes, such as livestock, feed, seed, and mechanical equipment.

Chapter 5
Resort Condominiums

Before we leave the realm of vacation retreats, let us consider two thoroughly modern concepts—the resort cooperative and the condominium. Both are currently in vogue in recreational areas, notably in such winter havens as Florida, Arizona, and even the islands of Hawaii and the Caribbean. They present another intriguing form of owning real estate for use and investment.

First we should have a clear understanding of both types of ownership, especially of the differences between them. Both are methods by which individuals own apartments in multi-family buildings. Both may consist of high-rise structures, low-rise garden apartments, clusters of town houses, or even huge complexes combining all of these designs. Most significant, in both cases, each occupant owns an individual equity in his own living quarters as well as a pro-rated interest in the common facilities, such as grounds, lobby, swimming pool, tennis courts, and the like. Financial responsibility for their maintenance is shared among the apartment owners. But there the similarity ends.

Now for the differences between the two concepts. Though cooperatives have been in vogue longer in the United States, condominiums actually date back to the Roman Empire and, having made their American debut during the 1950s, are rapidly becoming the more popular ownership format. Since they are in many ways less complex, let us go into them first, although we'll give examples of both later.

CONDOMINIUMS

Each resident literally owns his dwelling unit, exactly as if it were a one-family house. However, instead of getting a plot of land with it, he gets a shared ownership in the common areas and facilities of the complex.

He purchases his **condominium** from the original developer or the previous resident at a negotiated price and pays for it by any financing means that suit his needs. He can pay all cash for it or obtain a mortgage that meets his requirements.

If he sees fit to obtain a mortgage, he can choose his mortgage lender freely. If he is buying into a newly built condominium, the developer may offer a banking source from which he has a blanket mortgage commitment, much as does the builder of a one-family housing tract, but the purchaser need not use it.

In the course of his purchase, he obtains a title search and title insurance on his individual property. Real estate taxes are assessed against the value of his apartment and his share of the commonly owned property, proportionate to the size of his apartment. He is free to sell his unit when he chooses and to whom he chooses. And, subject to any restrictive covenants in his deed—and he does receive a deed when he buys a condominium—he can rent his premises to a tenant at any time. As in any community, of course, he is subject to the rules established by a committee of his peers.

Once he owns his apartment, the condominium resident pays interest and amortization on his mortgage, real estate taxes on his apartment, insurance, and interior maintenance just like the homeowner. However, he also pays a general maintenance charge to the condominium prorated, like the real estate taxes, according to the size of his apartment. This fee covers such common costs as grounds, lobby and elevator maintenance, heat and utilities, building services such as garbage removal and light repairs within the apartment, general insurance on the building itself, and payroll of the building staff.

COOPERATIVES

On the surface they may seem quite similar, but the principle of **cooperative** living is quite different. The co-op building—be it high- or low-rise or a combination of both—is owned by a corporation and operated under a corporate charter and by-laws. Residents in the building own shares of stock in the corporation. The number of shares owned by each tenant—and we must remember they are tenants—is proportionate to the value of his dwelling unit. Value, in this instance, is determined not only by the size of the apartment, but by its general desirability as affected by layout, height, location within the building, and the resultant view. Upon purchase of the required stock for a given apartment, the buyer also receives a proprietary lease under which he may occupy the premises.

60 *Real Estate for Use as Well as Investment*

Shares in a cooperative are generally bought for cash. The mortgage on the property is a single loan to the corporation on whatever terms the builder or the subsequent cooperative board of directors are able to negotiate. The shares owned by the tenants, taken together, represent the equity, or cash, investment in the property. The building is assessed for real estate taxes as a single entity and costs of insurance, maintenance and repairs, and other operating costs of running the building are also handled this way. The tenants in a cooperative, therefore, must pay monthly carrying charges that, taken together, will cover the monthly interest and amortization on the overall mortgage as well as the taxes and other costs involved. Each tenant's carrying charges reflect his proportionate share of the costs.

One could *almost* say that a co-op dweller plays the dual role of stockholder in a corporation which owns an apartment house in which he also happens to be a tenant, except for several considerations:

1. His tenancy is subject to the by-laws of the corporation, and these may prohibit subletting and almost certainly will require the board's approval of any sub-tenant.

2. He has no control over the amount of cash he pays down. The down payment, in the form of his stock purchase, is determined by the building's overall equity over the overall mortgage. If this requires too steep a cash payment, there are banks which offer personal loans to bridge the gap.

3. Because the size of the mortgage is beyond the tenant's control, so are the carrying charges, which bear a direct relationship to any seasonal rental he might wish to charge for a profitable investment.

So much for the differences in the two types of ownership.

ANTICIPATED INCOME—CONDOMINIUMS

Since we are discussing investment in a vacation residence, the best starting point is the condominium with its flexibility of financing. Suppose we have found an attractive two-bedroom apartment in Florida priced at $25,000, available for a $5,000 down payment. While we know that a twenty-five-year mortgage of $20,000 at 9½ percent interest (interest is usually higher for these properties) costs $174.74 a month, or $2,096.88 a year, this is relatively unimportant. What counts is the monthly carrying charges of $350 covering everything the building provides as well as the mortgage payments, for an annual total of $4,200. To make such an apartment attractive to prospective tenants will require an additional investment of, say, $5,000 in furnishings (though the basic appliances are usually provided by the developer as part of the purchase price). The total investment, therefore, is $10,000.

Even given the variables of resort life, such an apartment could com-

Resort Condominiums **61**

mand a monthly rental of $1,000 during the height of the winter season, taken to mean December 15 to March 15. Out of season, $500 a month will keep the apartment attractive to vacationers. The middle of the summer, July, August, and September, are generally unfavorable and the condominum owner should content himself with retrieving the $350 a month carrying charges for that period. In all, a fully rented apartment of this type should bring in an annual rent of about $7,000 against his carrying cost of $4,200. This suggests an annual return of $2,800, but let's be realistic. It is not the easiest task to keep such an apartment rented throughout the year, and if it were, it wouldn't leave any time for the owner to use it for his own pleasure. Nor does the $7,000 show brokers' fees and advertising to bring tenants, or the replacement of broken furnishings. Realistically, a *net* rental income of $5,200 a year, or a $1,000 profit, should suffice after all costs have been paid. Again, we can deduct the mortgage interest and real estate tax from the owner's personal income tax. Roughly speaking, these should total $2,400 in the first year, providing a tax saving of $600 to the investor in the 25 percent bracket. Thus, a truer measure of the return on a vacation condominium would be rent profit plus tax deductibility, for a total of $1,600, or 16 percent on $10,000 invested.

If, indeed, you do not anticipate using the apartment at all, you might do somewhat better by renting the unit to a single tenant for the entire year at $400 a month. This gives you a $600 cash profit plus the $600 tax benefit, for an assured total of $1,200, or a 12 percent return. You are also apt to save some money by avoiding multiple brokerage and advertising costs by finding a full-year tenant. Year-round tenants for winter condominiums come from two possible sources. First, there are permanent residents in Florida, Arizona, and other resort areas who need rental housing. Second, many couples planning retirement in the sun prefer to test their ultimate choice by taking a year's lease in a condominium in one of these resorts before buying. This is more likely the case in Florida or Arizona than in Hawaii or a Caribbean island.

ANTICIPATED INCOME—CO-OPS

Cooperatives are quite similar to condominiums in terms of return from rental income. But there are exceptions. The by-laws of a co-op corporation may prohibit certain rental practices. They may forbid you from leasing your apartment to more than one tenant in any calendar year, in which case you are restricted to a single full-year tenant, if you desire a full year's rental income. This would rule out the series of short-term tenancies we have discussed. Moreover, many co-op boards of directors reserve the right to approve your choice of tenant. In a condominium, as in a private house, you are the only judge of whom to accept as a tenant. In fact, some co-ops strive for a high degree of exclusivity by prohibiting *any* rentals. This type of cooperative would not lend itself to investment at all, except for your use and eventual resale at a profit.

As to resale, most co-ops demand the right to approve the new owner

62 *Real Estate for Use as Well as Investment*

and, in many cases, have the right of first refusal of your apartment if you do intend to sell it. This means that you must offer it back to the corporation at a stipulated price before you can even look for a purchaser.

LOCATION

On the resale of a condominium apartment, experience has shown startling increases in the values of condominiums in the more desirable resorts. Stories abound of purchasers whose apartments rose substantially in value even before the building was completed, impelling them to buy two or more extra units while work was still going on. Pitted against this we have the vagaries of local politics and the general economy. Racial or political unrest, as we have seen in some Caribbean islands, can quickly put a damper on the market for resort housing. And the moment the word "recession" appears in the headlines, the demand sags in Florida and Arizona at least temporarily. The same is true of resort areas with short seasons, such as the ski communities of Colorado, Nevada, and California. Even word of diminishing snow in successive years can thaw out what solid demand may have existed. To overcome this, developers are increasingly promoting such areas as year-round resorts, thus providing an added measure of stability.

A word of caution at this point. Regardless of politics, the economy, or changes in weather, the investor in a resort condominium should exercise considerable care. Unlike a secluded mountain or seaside cottage, a condominium is normally the creation of a developer who is operating in a competitive commercial climate. To maximize his own return on investment, he can be expected to advertise and promise something more than he will actually deliver. State and Federal laws effectively limit such abuses, especially as they apply to promises of the eventual resale value of the unit. Developers tend to continue to build in a favorable climate. As soon as your building has been finished and sold out, another may be put up to compete with it and thereby compete with you. This is why a resort apartment should not be purchased by an investor who lacks even a faint desire to ever live in it. If, however, retirement in, or at least seasonal use of, the apartment is at least a possibility, early purchase for investment is one of the best ways of getting there profitably.

Chapter 6
Stores and Offices

Perhaps the most sophisticated investment one can make for use and profit is that in one's own place of business. For one thing, the prices for commercial space and investments in commercial real estate are higher than almost any equivalent form of residential investment due to the higher cost of land in business districts. Also, there are so many different ways of making commercial investments, that it is impossible to illustrate all of them. However, we shall discuss two obvious versions: a merchant investing in a group of stores, and the professional in a small building with professional offices. An industrial building or a group of small plants are extensions of this, but such investments are likely to be beyond the means of most middle-income investors. In any case, the examples outlined here can be readily projected into other forms of commercial real estate.

Let's start with the stores. We first assume the investor has a viable retail business for which he needs a store so the comparison we will make here is between his cost in renting a store and that of owning a building with his and other shops in it. In so doing, we encounter several new principles of real estate economics which should be explained first.

Even though this is real estate for use and investment, we must abandon the concept used in residential examples in which we applied the income from the property to reducing the owner's cost of living in it. Here, we look at the real estate venture as a totally separate enterprise from that of the

64 *Real Estate for Use as Well as Investment*

retail business occupying it. The owner pays himself rent, just like his tenants. If he did not, he would have a thoroughly distorted picture of his retail operation, since rent is a basic expense. Indeed, he is best advised to establish a separate entity for the building, perhaps a partnership with his wife, a trust for his children, or were it not for corporate income taxes, even a corporation.

THE ECONOMICS

Here we encounter new types of mortgages. Unlike the mortgage on a home, the loan on the commercial building will not be completely self-amortizing over a term of many years. Instead, it will have a shorter term, and in the more common type of mortgage, the payments will cover all the interest but amortization of only part of the total. The remainder comes due all at once at the end of the shorter term. There are also **standing mortgages,** which call *only* for interest payments and no reduction of the principal through amortization—the entire amount comes due at the end. In our example, because it is more typical, we have chosen a ten-year loan with interest and some amortization, adding up to a constant annual payment. Though the owner may actually pay the lender in quarterly or monthly installments, it should be noted that in commercial real estate, not only costs but rentals as well are annualized, regardless of the payment schedule.

So much for the first mortgage. Now, we introduce the **second mortgage,** to make this type of investment even more viable for the investor. A second mortgage is a loan to reduce the amount of cash a purchaser of real estate must pay down. It is usually smaller than the first mortgage, has a shorter term, and is at higher interest because of its inherent risks. These risks we will discuss in a later chapter when we examine second mortgages as investments unto themselves. Suffice it to say that our merchant wishing to buy or build a property with several stores will need a second mortgage to make the deal possible. The **purchase money mortgage** is sometimes used in this context. A purchase money mortgage is a second mortgage, or loan, made by the seller of the property in order to make the sale feasible for the buyer. An ordinary second mortgage, on the other hand, is given by a third party, such as a financing company or institution.

In this discussion, also, we encounter new measures of real estate value. Whereas we look upon residential real estate in terms of rooms, commercial real estate values are largely determined by square-foot measure. There are two reasons for this. One is the fact that construction costs are calculated upon the basis of square-foot area. The other is simply the nature of commercial space, which can be put to many uses and partitioned in various ways, depending upon the user's needs. Consequently, the only available value determinant is the size of the area itself. There is one occasional exception: on shopping streets, the "front foot" is sometimes used instead as a measure. It refers to frontage facing the street. There is a good reason for this. It is the most important ingredient of retail space. The

Stores and Offices **65**

depth of the plot or store is secondary, simply because without a show window exposure of his wares to the shoppers' view, a merchant could not hope to entice the customers in.

Let us say that for his type of business our merchant needs a store with 30 feet of frontage and, to operate comfortably, a depth of 60 feet—a total of 1,800 square feet. Were he to rent in a thriving suburb or residential city neighborhood, this would cost him around $6 to $7 a square foot per year; if we take the figure of $6.67 this totals $12,000 annually.* Let's now assume he's contemplating building a structure to house his store and others just like it.

The selection (location) of a store property is not important here, because it is dictated primarily by the needs of merchants. If ours has found a location in which his retail business will thrive, he has probably found a spot where other stores should do equally well. In such a location, *land* might well have a market price of $1.67 a square foot, or $3,006 for the 1,800 feet. If this sounds inexpensive, consider it in terms of $100 a front foot, or $3,000 for the 30 total feet of frontage. This means that, for $100, each foot of street-front exposure belongs to him as long as he owns the property. This sounds like a fair price to pay for a chance to display his wares and provide an inviting entrance for shoppers. Not only does the front of his building serve as a wall with an entrance, but it doubles as exhibition space which, anywhere else, would cost a pretty penny.

Next comes the building itself. To be extremely conservative, let us say the one-story store structure can be built for approximately $20 a square foot or, in this instance $144,000 for a 7,200-square-foot building (four stores, 1,800 square feet each). This includes plumbing, heating, and electricity, and a small amount of partitioning, just enough to separate office and storage space from the selling area. Internal display fixtures, further partitioning for dressing rooms in a clothing store, and similar items are installed by each merchant and do not play a role here.

Thus, a 7,200-square-foot building ($144,000) on a 7,200-square-foot plot with 120 feet of frontage ($12,000) will cost $156,000, including land.

MORTGAGES

To finance this purchase (or construction) we begin with a first mortgage. In normal times, it should not be difficult to obtain a mortgage that covers 60 percent of the total value, or $93,600. Such a loan will probably have a term of ten years and call for constant annual payments of 12 percent. Let's look at the constant payment. Since this is a commercial property, with risks greater than those of a private house (the owner could go out of business) the interest rate might well be 10 percent a year. The remaining 2 percent of the constant annual payment goes toward reduction of the principal. What is left of the principal when the loan matures is known as the **balloon.**

*We could, at this point, illustrate why his landlord would charge this rent, but this will become apparent when we show why a group of stores is a good investment for him.

66 *Real Estate for Use as Well as Investment*

If, then, we were to finance the $156,000 property with a first mortgage of $93,600, we would face a cash down payment of $62,400, but this is hard to come by. The solution lies in a **second mortgage.** It should be possible to obtain a second mortgage for $32,400, thus reducing the cash investment to a more convenient $30,000. Second mortgages, however, entail even greater risks to the lender for reasons we will deal with in a later chapter. Therefore he will limit the term of the second mortgage to, say, five years and assume a much higher interest rate, say, 15 percent. This will probably be a **standing mortgage,** one which the property buyer will not amortize. He will simply pay 15 percent interest on the $32,400, or $4,860 a year. When the second mortgage matures five years hence, he must have reserved $32,400 from his rental income so he can pay it all off.

Now let's review the financial structure of this property.*

THE FIRST FIVE-YEAR PERIOD

Land for 4 stores, 120 X 60 feet at $100 per front foot	$ 12,000
Structure containing 7,200 square feet at $20 per square foot	144,000
Total property cost (excluding legal and sundries)	$156,000
or	or
1st mortgage, 10-year at 12% constant annual payment	93,600
2nd mortgage, 5-year term at 15% straight interest	32,400
Cash investment (down payment)	30,000
	$156,000

Assuming the 7,200-square-foot building is ready to be rented, or is already rented at $6.67 a square foot per year, the following will be the annual income and expense budget for the *first five* years:

Now, before you are tempted to spend the $9,608, remember that in five years, you have a deadline to repay in full the second mortgage of $32,400. This means you should set aside 20 percent of the principal, or $6,480, each year, starting now. This will leave you with a net yield of $3,128 for each of the first five years, or an annual return before taxes of 10.4 percent on your investment of $30,000. We should mention here that the $6,480 set aside each year for repayment of the second mortgage can be invested meanwhile. It can be placed in a savings account. The owner can purchase government bonds or some other interest-paying instrument and thereby earn additional money at a rate of about 6 percent.

Now let us look at the property at the end of the first five years, and at what happens during the second five years.

The second mortgage has been paid off and the interest on it is removed

---

*In all our projections, we have used static rents, taxes, and maintenance costs for the full term of ownership. Clearly this is not consonant with real-life economics. Taxes, heating fuel, utilities, and many other items tend to change with time—usually upward. But so should the rents the investor charges his tenants. How this is accomplished is explained at the end of this chapter.

Stores and Offices   67

	EXPENSES	INCOME
Rent (including owner's own store rent paid to property) (7,200 feet at $6.67)		$48,000
Interest and amortization on 1st mortgage (12% of $93,600)	$11,232	
Interest on 2nd mortgage (15% of $32,400)	4,860	
Taxes (commercial property is probably assessed at 50% of true value, or $78,000, and tax rate is assumed to be $15 per $100 of assessed valuation)	11,700	
Heat and utilities	3,600	
Maintenance and provision for vacancies	7,000	
Total expenses	$38,392	
Gross profit		$ 9,608

from the expense budget. The first mortgage (of $93,600) has been brought down 10 percent to $84,240 by the 2 percent per year amortization paid over the initial five years. It will come down a like amount by the end of the second five, leaving a balloon of $74,880 to be paid off at that time.

THE SECOND FIVE-YEAR PERIOD

	EXPENSES	INCOME
Rent from four stores remains at		$48,000
Interest and amortization on 1st mortgage (12% constant)	$11,232	
Taxes (assuming same assessment and tax rate)	11,700	
Heat and utilities	3,600	
Maintenance and provision for vacancies	7,000	
Total expenses	$33,532	
Gross profit		14,468
To be set aside (and invested for repayment on the "balloon" on the first mortgage)		10,868
At this point, the owner can take home a 12% yield on his $30,000 investment each year, and use it at his pleasure.		3,600

The investor is earning an annual yield of 12 percent of his original $30,000 investment. By the end of the ninth year, he has recaptured the $30,000 itself ($3,128 each year for the first five years is $15,640; $3,600 each for the next five years is $18,000). In addition, he can count on some interest income from the $10,868 set aside each year for repayment of the first mortgage. At straight 5 percent interest, the four-year income amounts to $2,173.60 and there will be more from the subsequent annual sums set aside. We recommend that this again be held aside for vacancies and other contingencies and not considered as part of the property's income.

68 *Real Estate for Use as Well as Investment*

Where does that leave the property at the end of ten years? The first mortgage has now been paid down to a balloon of $74,880. In addition, we set aside a total of $54,340 over the second five years. With this we can deflate the balloon quite a bit, but still owe the mortgage lender $20,540. To repay it, as he must at this point, the investor can obtain a *new* first mortgage of $21,000 on the property, same as he did on the *extra land* (page 42). This time he should take a five-year, self-amortizing mortgage, similar to the one on a private house. At an interest rate of 10 percent a year, a self-amortizing $21,000, five-year loan calls for annual payments of $5,355.

THE THIRD FIVE-YEAR PERIOD

	EXPENSES	INCOME
Rent		$48,000
Interest and amortization on new 1st mortgage, less expenses	$ 5,355	
Taxes (assuming no change)	11,700	
Heat and utilities	3,600	
Maintenance and provision for vacancies	7,000	
Total expenses	$27,655	
Net yield (since there is no need for further setting aside an amortization reserve)		20,345

The yield (of $20,345) has increased to 67.8 percent per year on the $30,000 originally invested!

After the fifteenth year, assuming no changes in rent, taxes, etc., the new mortgage is also paid off, thus decreasing annual expenses by its cost of $5,355, and increasing the yield by a like amount, to $25,700, or 85.6 percent on the $30,000 invested fifteen years earlier.

Altogether the property has paid the investor back well through the years of ownership, thus enabling him to make new investments elsewhere or merely to enjoy the fruits of his patience.

So much for tangible income. But we also have **cash flow,** as explained in our discussion of vacation homes. Cash flow, we remember, is the total of cash and noncash income. The noncash portion is the depreciation of the property which actually does not depreciate materially. Let us take the building with the four stores. It cost $144,000 to build or buy, not counting the land, which does not depreciate. If the structure is deemed to have a useful life of fifty years from the date of construction or purchase, it means that the investor can allocate 2 percent, or $2,880 toward depreciation each year. This is not money he can use, or even gets to see. However, the taxable income from the property is reduced by that amount, thus saving him (or his partnership or trust) a proportionate amount of income taxes.

There is, of course, another side to this coin. Let us assume that he sells the property for $180,000 ten years after purchase. Since he paid $156,000 for it, this suggests a capital gain of $24,000. But he depreciated the

Stores and Offices **69**

structure by $28,800 ($2,880 a year for ten years) so his cost base of the property has come down from $156,000 to $127,200. Hence, in the eyes of the tax authorities, his taxable capital gain in the $180,000 sale is $52,800 not $24,000. But there is an advantage to doing this. The capital gains tax on $52,800 is still less than what the total might have been of ordinary income tax on the annual $2,880 (had he not taken depreciation) and capital gains tax on the $24,000. What is more the tax becomes payable at a far more convenient time—when the final profit is actually taken in. In effect, the investor has been able to use the property's cash flow to pay himself his annual income from the building and postpone the taxes on the depreciation portion of it.

The physician, dentist, or other professional may also choose to buy or build a building with professional offices and no stores. The economics of this type of venture are the same as those of the building containing stores. However, if the professional office building is not located on a shopping street, the land cost is most likely calculated on a square-foot rather than a front-foot basis. Depending upon the locality, it will represent similar values.

Now that we have the basic idea, it is easy to extend the example of the four stores (or offices) as far as you want to go. Take, to start with, a *two-story* building of the same size, one hundred twenty by sixty feet. The street floor of 7,200 square feet contains the four retail establishments. The upstairs space, an additional 7,200 square feet, is earmarked for offices. This combination might appeal to either a retail merchant or a businessman or professional with office-space requirements. This means the investor would occupy one of the street-floor stores or a part of the second-floor office space.

If zoning permits such a structure, the cost of the land might be about the same—$12,000. To be very conservative, let us postulate that construction costs remain at $20 per square foot, for a total of about $300,000. Actually it should be slightly less, since there is need for only one foundation, one roof, one somewhat larger heating plant, and so forth. Some of the savings might be offset by need for added partitioning and sanitary facilities. Ordinarily, the landlord provides only basic office layouts, including walls and doors. Extensive interior improvements can usually be charged to tenants. The upstairs office rent can also be figured at $6.67 a square foot on a gross area basis. **Gross area,** a new term in these discussions, is the total of the space actually occupied by each tenant plus his proportionate share of the area taken up by public halls, lavatories, stairwells, and the like. **Net usable area,** on the other hand, is the space actually occupied. Therefore, if the net rent is, say, $6 a square foot and the public areas represent 10 percent of the interior space, the tenant should be charged $6.60 per square foot of usable area. Either way, the end result should be exactly the same.

This concept does not contemplate the cost of an elevator. Indeed, if neighborhood competition makes an elevator advisable, it may also be even wiser to think in terms of going to a three-story structure, if zoning

70 *Real Estate for Use as Well as Investment*

permits. We are then talking about a 21,600-square-foot building, at a construction cost of $35 a square foot, because of the elevator and fire stairs (probably mandatory under many building codes) for a total of $756,000. Land for this type of development might also cost more. Instead of $12,000 for a one-story retail building, it might be worth as much as $20,000. We are now in the realm of a $776,000 piece of real estate.

A project of this sort would probably command a first mortgage equal to 60 percent of the total value, or $465,600, which means a down payment of $310,400. To reduce the cash investment further, a second mortgage of $150,000 could probably be found. That leaves $160,400 of cash to be invested and probably calls for a partnership of several like-minded investors. This brings us to the door of real estate syndication, a subject involving rules of its own, which we take up in detail in a later chapter.

Before we leave the discussion of retail or office buildings for use and investment, we should consider the probabilities. Remember, the possible increases in costs that are to be offset by increases in rent. These are ways the investor/landlord can provide for this:

1. By making his leases with his tenants for relatively short terms, such as five years, he can raise rents upon renewal in accordance with his increased taxes and other carrying costs.

2. He can write leases of any duration with "escalation" clauses. Under the terms of such clauses, the rent can be raised each year in proportion to increased building operating costs, provided the investor, as landlord, documents his higher costs for the tenants.

3. With retail tenants only, the investor, or landlord, can agree upon **percentage leases.** Instead of charging $12,000 a year for a thirty-by-sixty-foot store, he may charge slightly less, say $10,000, but the lease provides that if the tenant's total business volume exceeds a specified amount, let us say $80,000 a year, the rent goes up 2 percent, or $200, for every $1,000 of additional volume. So if the store does $100,000 in a given year, for instance, the "percentage" yield would be $4,000, for a total rent of $14,000. This gives the landlord a small "piece of the action" in his tenant's retail business. More importantly, it hedges the landlord, or investor, against inflation. For if *his* costs rise with inflation, so should the dollar volume of a retail store, if properly run. Bear in mind, too, that the investor's lease with himself, for his own store, should have similar provisions for the sake of his real estate venture as well as that of his store operation.

There are other probabilities. The examples we have worked with in this discussion assume certain prices for land, construction, and consequently, a rental of $6.67 a square foot. Needless to say, these factors vary with each

Stores and Offices **71**

community and, indeed, from one shopping street to the next. Obviously, if land and building values are higher or lower, by virtue of neighborhood conditions, rents will vary commensurately. Construction costs, of course, would be the same within the same general geographic area, though they will rise proportionately with inflation. This only points up the folly of erecting a new retail building in a run-down neighborhood. But then the investor would not want to build his own new store there, either.

There is no provision here, either, for business cycles or declining neighborhoods. A recession of major proportions or blight of any area may force retail tenants to close their shops, leaving the investor with vacancies. While we put in a modest provision for vacancies and replacing tenants, this contingency does entail brokers' commissions or even loss of income for a period of time. There is, after all, no investment venture without risk.

If the investor is considering construction of a retail or retail-and-office building, he must also obtain a construction loan. The mortgages described in our examples are known in the real estate industry as **take-outs.** They become available to be taken out only when the building is finished. In fact, most lending institutions will not make a commitment for a permanent mortgage until the investor-builder can demonstrate that he has enough tenants signed up whose rents suffice to pay the taxes and mortgage obligation. In other words, if the first mortgage calls for an annual payment of $11,232 and taxes of $11,700 (as in our first example), a prospective mortgage lender will want to see two stores rented to stable retailers at a total of $24,000, to feel secure in making the loan. The investor's own store, if in a reasonably secure line of merchandising, can serve as one of these. Given such evidence of income, the banks, insurance companies, and other lending institutions will make a commitment for a first mortgage. It may be advantageous for the investor to shop for a mortgage through a real estate or mortgage broker, but he can begin his search with his local banker.

Once he has such a "take-out" commitment for a permanent mortgage, he can apply to a commercial bank for a construction loan for part of the cost of erecting the building. In the example used at the outset, with $30,000 to be invested, the first $12,000 is used to purchase the land. The remaining $18,000 must be held available for construction to supplement the construction loan. If the investor can obtain a short-term mortgage of $6,000 on the land, he can add this to the funds available for construction, too. Construction loans are paid out piecemeal to match the payments due the building contractor. Generally, an investor in a building venture should not attempt to work without the services of a lawyer, and he can rely on his attorney to arrange the details of the temporary and permanent financing for him.

FINDING TENANTS

This is another probability to be reckoned with. Much depends upon the location. If an investor buys an existing building, perhaps the one in which

72 *Real Estate for Use as Well as Investment*

he already operates a store, he will automatically assume the leases of the tenants in possession. If he is building a new set of four stores, he has several avenues to find tenants. In some thriving locations, a mere sign announcing the construction of new stores will bring both direct tenant inquiries as well as brokers with prospective tenants. Elsewhere, an investor had best list his property with brokers who specialize in store rentals. Newspaper advertising can also be very effective. A combination of all three should bring good results for both original tenants and replacements in case of vacancies. An astute owner will also track the performance of his tenants' stores as closely as possible. Thus he should not be caught unprepared if a tenant plans to close his business or move it. Obviously, the earlier he seeks a replacement, the smaller will be his risk of losing rental income. Stores and offices simply cannot be rented as quickly as apartments.

It may seem we have given too much attention to stores and offices for use and investment, but we have done so because as investments their analysis can be projected into virtually all types of commercial real estate. The budgets we have examined are similar to the **set-ups** rendered by professional investors and brokers when they offer properties for sale, or seek to obtain mortgages from prospective lenders. The principles, with many variations and added complexities, remain the same—even for the owner of a skyscraper.

PART III

REAL ESTATE FOR ACTIVE INVESTMENT

INTRODUCTION

Now that we have examined the investment potential of properties that we use in our daily lives, let us turn to the more professional aspects of investing in real estate. There is nothing intimidating about the term professional in this context, for it is merely the notion that real estate ownership is an investment that is independent of the place in which we live or work. Many of the principles are the same as in private investment: real estate still consists of land and buildings and is financed with cash and mortgage loans; there is rental income; we pay taxes and interest on mortgages; and we are responsible for property maintenance, to one degree or another. Most important, we have an opportunity to derive income from property and, upon resale, should realize a capital gain. The investor, however, is now called upon to negotiate more shrewdly, consider a greater number of potential risks, and, in general, must become somewhat more involved in the management of his assets in realty.

Chapter 7
Land Investments

Since land is the basic commodity from which all real estate concepts spring, let us begin here. As we have already seen in the example cited in chapter 2 of the home with extra lots, the primary objective of a land investment is the **capital gain** upon its resale. With some exceptions, which we will also explore, there is little one can do with vacant land while it is being held for resale. Essentially, land ownership is regarded as a sound hedge against inflation and a positive bet on the future growth of our population and the economy. Needless to say, an economic downturn can affect land values negatively, but the hazards are far smaller than those of more volatile investments, especially during a time when there is a virtual certainty that inflation will continue for an indefinite period.

Land investments can take two basic forms. First, a prospective investor can independently select a parcel (piece) of land in almost any area. Second, he can invest in land in one of the many land development projects offered by companies specializing in the propagation of new communities. Both have their inherent advantages, as well as their risks.

CHOOSING A LOT

If you decide to buy a parcel of land on your own, you should begin with a careful investigation of where to make your investment. There are many options open to you, but as a general rule, you should steer clear of any

76 *Real Estate for Active Investment*

areas with which you are not familiar, and, instead, limit your search to those areas whose characteristics and growth potential you understand clearly.

For the astute real estate investor (the full-time professional), the search for good land investment is no problem. He can devote time and money in an investigation of vacant land hundreds of miles from where he lives and works. The part-time investor, however, must rely on more readily available information. This is why it is better to limit our discussion to familiar surroundings.

Start with your own community. This could be the suburb in which you live, your particular neighborhood within a city or simply the general environment in which you have worked long enough to become thoroughly acquainted with it. Since we are considering relatively small investments, a residential neighborhood offers many worthwhile opportunities. A walk through a neighborhood may well reveal vacant lots between homes which you may have ignored in the past. There is probably a reason why there are no homes built on them. It may simply be that nobody has chosen to buy them and build on them. However, they may still be vacant because of a serious defect, such as a drainage problem, an **easement** which is irreconcilable with any future development. The view may be unattractive, or the lot may border a garbage dump that is not readily seen from the street. Or they may be zoned unfavorably because they are not large enough to accommodate a house under the local code. For example, local zoning may require that each house on that street needs a plot with sixty feet of street frontage, and this lot has only fifty-eight. But, it is just as likely that it is being held for investment by a nearby homeowner, much as we described in the preceding chapter.

This is not intended to sound negative. I am merely pointing up the basic question we must ask ourselves when considering an investment in vacant land: why is it vacant when other parcels near it aren't? The answer to this simple question is, perhaps, the most important aspect of an intelligent decision to invest in land.

Now let us look at the affirmative side: communities tend to grow. This single fact offsets the negatives and is the basic premise of investment in land, whether residential or commercial. Determining how and in which direction they will grow is fundamental to decision making and investment. Therefore, land parcels adjacent to the newest residential frontier are likely to become the next area to be developed. But some degree of logic must prevail. Growth is not necessarily uniform around the community's perimeter. A shopping center planned on one side of town may act as a stimulant or as a deterrent. It may invite people to build their homes closer to it, or it may encourage only commercial and industrial development, thereby forcing residential development toward the more rural side of town. In either case, plans for a shopping center suggest that growth is anticipated. The fact that a major investor, not to mention the large retail chains who will probably be taking space, is betting on the growth of the community, is a strong indication that investment in the area is thriving.

The age of the population is another clue. I can think of numerous neighborhoods whose original population is slowly dying out. The homes, built during the early part of the century, have no discernible future except as rooming houses or as homes for a disadvantaged element of the population. A vacant lot in such a neighborhood has little future for residential development, nor would it support a new store. However, we need not totally disregard them: obsolete neighborhoods tend to attract commercial and industrial development, largely because the land is inexpensive, even with the added cost of razing the existing buildings. On the other hand, a community with a young population attracts younger, more affluent people, and with them comes an influx of high-grade retail and other commercial development.

How can you gather information like this about an area? The safest way is to confine your search to the community in which you have lived for some years; this knowledge has already become second nature to you without your even being aware of it.

The same is true of recreational areas. Remember the mountain cabin or cottage by the seashore we discussed earlier? Once you have lived there for awhile, made friends who also know the environment, and explored the vicinity as part of your vacation fun, you will begin to have a fairly accurate judgment of its future. You will get word of how the local motels are faring, or if there are plans to develop a resort nearby. You should hear of these developments sooner than the outsider, and become, in fact, an insider.

You have access to some of the same information about the neighborhood where you work. Each working day you can observe the economic health of your business surroundings, be they commercial or industrial. A store or restaurant doing brisk business and expanding from time to time is a good sign. An empty store or one with a continual change of tenants is a warning. Even the particular type of occupancy in a store has its meaning. The owner of a junkyard may, indeed, get wealthy, but junkyards do not gravitate to burgeoning neighborhoods. Nor do automobile body repair shops or stores that sell remnants.

THE ECONOMICS

What, then, are the viable land investments for the middle-income investor, and what are his prospects for an attractive return? Let us begin with a parcel in a residential neighborhood where reasonably new middle-income houses prevail. A home in this area should be valued at $36,000, comprising a plot worth $6,000 and a structure with a current replacement value of $30,000. Let us assume, therefore, that you are offered a piece of land which will accommodate six homes for $36,000.

First you must ascertain whether the land will, indeed, allow for construction of six houses. This means you will have to research the zoning regulations which determine the amount of land area or square footage

78 *Real Estate for Active Investment*

required for each house. In addition, the zoning regulations usually stipulate a minimum amount of front footage per house and the required depth of a building lot. Moreover, they specify what type of construction is permitted on a particular piece of land.

Supposing, then, that the available land is usable for residential construction, and therefore the investor can begin negotiating with the seller. Before discussing price, it is wise to find out why he is offering the land for sale. Whatever his answer, it should be verified through outside sources. A real estate broker in your own community—notably the one who may have brought you together with the prospective seller—can be helpful. Your lawyer, too, can help you gather this information. After all, there could be impediments such as **easements** upon the property which might impede future development. An easement is a deeded right by which an outside party—public or private—may encroach upon the property for one purpose or another. For example, the owner of the land parcel behind the one you are considering may have a perpetual right or easement to build or maintain an access driveway right through the spot on which your house may be built. Or, a sewer authority or a utility company could maintain an easement at a critical point for its conduits, thus rendering the land useless for construction. These possibilities should be determined before serious negotiations begin. However, they will probably come to light during the title search which precedes the title closing, or conveyance of the deed, which is necessary to complete the transaction.

CLEAR TITLE

This is a good time to acquaint the investor with the importance of a clear title. Actually, this discussion pertains to every piece of real property—a home, condominium, store or office building—as well as vacant land. But since land is being examined here as the most basic realty commodity, title is now a critical consideration. It is the title to the land which is the primary consideration in any title search.

Obviously, one cannot sell something which one does not own. And, by the same token, there is a degree of jeopardy for the buyer of land that a seller does not completely own. In real estate, the history of the title is the clue to true ownership. Therefore, when one considers purchasing a piece of land, one must make certain in advance that the seller's statements of ownership are true, even beyond his best knowledge and belief. To accomplish this, one usually turns to a title company whose business it is to research records, usually maintained by the County Clerk or a similar official, to determine the passage of the deed through various hands throughout the past decades—or even centuries. A title company will institute such a search for a reasonable fee, usually not more than $200, and then render a report. A report of this kind will show through whose hands ownership of the land has passed, virtually from the first settler or claimant to the property up to the present. It will indicate whether the property was

Land Investments **79**

ever pledged as collateral for a mortgage or other kind of indebtedness, and whether or not this pledge was ultimately redeemed through repayment of the loan. If there have ever been any disputes over the ownership—between members of a feuding family or as a result of a lawsuit—the title search should reveal it. It will even uncover that rare situation where title may have once been vested in the three sons of a previous owner. If one of these heirs then disappeared, even decades ago, his sudden reappearance, or that of his heirs, may cast a cloud upon the title—hence the term "clouded title"—unless there are documents proving that his branch of the family subsequently renounced its rights to the part-ownership of the property. A title company, once convinced that the title is completely clear, will write a title insurance policy. For a modest one-time premium, which includes the search fee, this policy assures the new owner that if some claimant suddenly looms out of nowhere to claim all or part of the ownership, his rightful claim will be paid by the insurance company, including the cost of litigation needed to settle the matter.

The cost of title searches and insurance varies. If, for example, no recent title search has been documented by the same title company, the search may have to delve back to the days of the Indians and early settlers. This is obviously more expensive than a search which begins with the present owner or his immediate predecessor. The latter is much easier, since it begins with a valid search which has already brought the property's ownership to within the last owner or two. However, even so recent a search could unearth a **lien** against the property, that might arise from unpaid real estate taxes or other debts. In some parts of the United States, the **Torrens system** is in effect. This is a recording method by which the local authorities track the title and any liens against it on a continuing basis. The Torrens system makes a certification of clear title a relatively quick and inexpensive procedure.

NEGOTIATIONS

Returning, however, to the investment in the residential land parcel, let us take a closer look at the negotiations. Here, again, we can apply the same methods of bargaining that precede the purchase of any kind of real estate discussed so far in this book. You can assume that the seller is going to ask more for the property than he expects to get. You will normally offer less than you are prepared to pay. After a number of such offers and bids, each hopefully narrowing the gap, you should arrive at a mutually satisfactory price. Regardless of how one finds an available land parcel—through a real estate broker, a *For Sale* sign, a newspaper advertisement—it is certain that the prospective seller has already established an asking price. One never knows in advance how close to the real market value that asking price may be. Some owners prefer to be realistic. Their asking price may be only slightly higher than what they will finally accept. Others demand a much higher sum just for openers, and are prepared to yield considerably during

80 *Real Estate for Active Investment*

negotiations. In any case, an investor should *not* accede to the first asking price, if for no other reason than to test the tenacity of the seller. If a broker is involved, one can usually obtain a fairly reliable indication of how much the seller will come down from his stated price tag. And, since we are recommending that the investor in vacant land look for something in his own community, he should have a fairly accurate estimate of what it is worth. Perhaps the best way to indicate what the investor will ultimately pay for his land is to invoke the classic definition of **market value** in real estate parlance. By this definition, market value is the price arrived at between a willing buyer and a willing seller, neither under any compulsion to buy or sell and both knowing the best and highest use of the property. From this definition, it becomes obvious that a seller in financial distress might accept something less than the market value of a property. This may provide an unusual opportunity for an investor, but such bargains are relatively rare, especially in an inflationary economy. As for the best and highest use, it becomes irrelevant here. Suffice it to say that should the buyer know, and the seller *not* know that there is a special advantage attached to the property—oil underground or a major government center to be built nearby—the negotiated price would not reflect true market value.

By now, we should have arrived at the market value of $36,000 for the residential parcel we will discuss. Once the investor has shaken hands with the seller on a sale at a fixed price, a contract of sale should be drawn up by their respective lawyers. At the time the contract is signed, the investor is normally expected to deposit 10 percent, or $3,600 as good-faith or **earnest money.** This money, under most contracts, is returnable to the buyer if the seller cannot deliver clear title to the property. On the other hand, the buyer agrees to forfeit the deposit if, for reasons of his own making, he does not go through with the purchase. Such default would occur if, for example, he failed to raise the additional $32,400, or even if he simply changed his mind about the deal. Also, at the time of contract signing, the two parties set the date for the title closing—the conveyance of the deed to the new owner. In the interim, the investor should institute the title search and arrange for a title insurance policy to be issued at the time of closing. During that period, usually a month to six weeks, the investor must also secure a mortgage if he doesn't intend to pay all cash for the land. Mortgages on vacant land are more difficult to obtain than those on owner-occupied houses or on income-producing commercial property because it has no immediate utility except resale potential. However, a local bank might be disposed to provide a mortgage covering 50 percent, or $18,000, of the price. This is contingent, of course, upon the mortgage banker's concurrence that $36,000 is, indeed, the true market value of the land. This is an important reason why market value is such a critical concept: mortgage appraisals must support it, and vice versa.

On the day of the title closing, the investor arrives at the meeting with his certified check for $14,400 ($18,000 less the $3,600 he paid over when the contract was signed). The mortgage lender brings a check for $18,000, the

Land Investments **81**

note and mortgage documents. The representative of the title insurance company holds a policy to cover the new owner against claims. And the seller brings the deed. By the time they leave the room, the seller has a total of $32,400, consisting of a certified check of $14,400 given to him by the new owner, and a check of $18,000 from the mortgage lender. This together with the $3,600 deposit, gives him the sale price of $36,000. The banker leaves with a signed note and mortgage, evidencing the investor's debt to him. The title insurance man departs with a check from the investor covering the cost of title search and the one-time premium for the insurance policy. Each of the lawyers collects his stipend from his respective client. And the investor walks away with a deed to the property.

POTENTIAL RETURNS

Now that you have witnessed a $36,000 investment in a piece of land, let us look at its potential for yielding a return. When we discussed other types of property for use and investment, we looked at their resale value as a by-product. Essentially, we were interested in the annual income the investment created in one form or another. In fact, when we talked about reselling the extra lot, we assumed that an increase in value was merely commensurate with the 10 percent rate of inflation.

Were this to be true of the $36,000 piece of vacant land, it would bring $72,000 after ten years, or a net of $54,000 after repaying the mortgage of $18,000. This is a hedge against inflation. (In today's parlance, a hedge against inflation is an investment in any commodity whose market price is likely to rise in direct proportion to inflation, even though its intrinsic and market values remain the same.) But how much of a hedge? The $18,000 mortgage, probably a **standing mortgage** which is not amortized, required the payment of, say, 9½ percent interest, or $1,710 a year, for a total of $17,100 during the ten-year period. The property, assessed at the typical one-third of true value, or $12,000, might have commanded annual real estate taxes of $10 per $100 of the assessed valuation. This comes to $1,200 a year, or a total of $12,000 over ten years. In other words, the taxes and mortgage interest will have cost the investor $29,100, over and above the $36,000 purchase price, just to carry the property during his ownership. This leaves him with a net taxable capital gain of $6,900. Under present income tax laws, he would have to pay a 25 percent capital gains tax of $1,725, leaving him $5,175 as profit. Pro-rated over ten years, his return would have been $517.50, or 2.8 percent a year. Even after taxes, this is clearly unsatisfactory.

It should, therefore, be obvious that there must be an added variable in making a sensible investment in vacant land. For lack of a better word, that variable can be defined as *prescience*. One must have a solid feeling that the vacant land, if held for a certain period of time, will increase in value and have greater utility than it did when it was purchased. How does one know this?

82 *Real Estate for Active Investment*

One answer is to observe the dwindling supply of land in a given residential neighborhood. As the community grows, it should become increasingly difficult to find buildable residential lots close to the center of town. Given such an appreciation in value, it might well be possible to sell the $36,000 parcel of land for $72,000 after only five years. Remember that at the rate of 10 percent a year inflation alone will bring the value to $54,000. The remainder of the increment then represents that prescience, foreknowledge of rising land values. Selling the land for $72,000 after five years means that the investor paid only five years' interest, or $8,550, and only five years' real estate taxes, or $6,000, for total carrying charges of $14,550. Thus, after repaying the $18,000 principal of the mortgage, his gross profit on his $18,000 investment is $21,450. The capital gains tax on this is about $5,362.50, leaving an after-tax profit of $16,087.50. In other words, the property yielded $3,217.50 each of the five years it was held, which is a return of 17.9 percent after taxes. It should always be remembered that since the income is not taken upon a yearly basis and the capital gains tax has already been figured into this calculation, the 17.9 percent is not subject to income tax. By any standard, this is a handsome yield.

Even if there is a change in the neighborhood structure, including a seemingly adverse one, the investment might still be valid. Perhaps the area is no longer desirable for one-family homes. If apartment buildings or commercial enterprises are beginning to encroach on the neighborhood, vacant land can bring an even more attractive return. Developers are prepared to pay a good price for vacant land which can be used to create income-producing real estate on a large scale. In fact, you may find yourself considering the role of developer in your own right if, in ten years, your resources permit.

An investment in vacant land, therefore, is akin to buying a relatively stable commodity, keeping it on the shelf until the demand increases and reselling it at precisely the right moment to obtain the optimum price for it.

Your land, however, need not sit idly by while the tax collector and mortgage lender take your money. If zoning permits, you can rent it to a parking-lot operator for at least the carrying charges. It may even be possible to permit some inexpensive construction, such as a service station or repair shop. This, of course, would be permissible only in neighborhoods which are not totally residential, and it is in just such a neighborhood that temporary improvements serve their best purpose. If a once-residential neighborhood is on the decline, the next logical turn would be toward the commercial or industrial. In this case, there would normally be a demand for both parking space as well as for supportive facilities such as service and repair shops. If, at the optimum moment, the land can be resold profitably, demolition of an existing structure such as a gasoline station is not a prohibitive expense. In these instances, of course, the lease must have a short enough term to provide the lot owner with enough flexibility to sell his property when he deems the time to be right. This type of agreement works both ways. Anyone putting up a service facility on the basis of a short-term lease is not apt to construct a very substantial building.

LAND INVESTMENT IN RESORT AREAS

Land investment in resort areas follows the same principles, but here your judgment must be somewhat keener. While you may enjoy your vacation cottage in a given locale, it does not always mean that droves of city folk will become infected with the same yen for spending their leisure days in your favorite retreat. Yet, there is considerable evidence that many people will. Investors who purchased land in the now-popular ski areas of Vermont, New Hampshire, California, and Colorado have enjoyed handsome returns on their investments. Their parcels are being bought by like-minded ski-enthusiasts and by developers of motels, resort hotels and condominiums. Growth in such areas has, in fact, been rather rapid. Investments have matured in ten years or less.

Then there are areas much closer to the big cities—Connecticut, the Pocono Mountains of Pennsylvania, the hills of Virginia, or the lake country of Wisconsin—where people from New York, Philadelphia, Washington, or Chicago can build weekend and summer homes. However, where there is no well-defined resort development either in progress or at least on the horizon, the maturing of a land investment must be figured at a much longer range. It might well be the type of investment a father could pass on to his children as a worthwhile asset.

COMMERCIAL OR INDUSTRIAL LAND

The forces of supply and demand become even more pronounced in the selection of commercial or industrial land. Here again we would caution *against* an investment unless there is either a clear trend of development or a careful study of the area's economic profile. Undoubtedly, fortunes have been made through land investments along major roads surrounding cities, areas which clearly invited industrial parks, shopping centers and the like. Oddly enough, such land can be bought at surprisingly low prices before growth trends are apparent to most people. But urban areas have a way of reneging on their promises. And while the east end of town may have been the logical center for industrial development, one successful industrial park on the west side may turn the tide in the opposite direction. For this reason, it is best to be prepared to pay a little more for a vacant parcel; payment, in effect, for the privilege of waiting for major development to begin in the area of your choice.

The cost of guessing wrong in vacant land investment is not necessarily prohibitive. Barring some outlandishly adverse turn of events, it is usually possible to sell a parcel of land for its original price or close to it. The loss can therefore be held to little more than the cost of carrying the mortgage and paying the taxes. After all, land is a relatively stable commodity.

84 *Real Estate for Active Investment*

TAX LIENS

In view of its stability, vacant land sometimes offers a special bonanza to an astute investor with limited funds to spend. This is the purchase of **tax liens.** Admittedly, in the face of inflation, opportunities for this type of purchase are rapidly diminishing, but with sufficient alertness, they can be found. Let us now examine the principle of tax liens.

If the owner of a property defaults upon his payments of real estate taxes, the municipality or county has the right to foreclose. In simple terms, this means that the local government repossesses a property on which taxes are substantially in arrears. Since, in most instances, the town or village or county do not have any immediate use for the land, the authorities place these properties on the auction block to recover the unpaid taxes. In some cases, these properties are literally auctioned off, with the outstanding taxes as a minimum or "upset" price. In other jurisdictions, the properties are offered for sale at exactly the amount of the taxes due plus the government's cost of foreclosing and handling the sale.

The question arises, therefore, whether the entire property is worth as much as the unpaid taxes. If the property in default includes a building, this could, indeed, be a serious question. After all, if it is a home in an attractive neighborhood, the owner should have been able to sell it for enough money to meet his tax obligation. If he could not, it is ample testimony to the undesirable nature of the area. In the case of a commercial or industrial building, the mere fact that the property did not yield the owner enough to pay his taxes, thereby forcing him to abandon it, should be the fatal warning signal.

Land, however, is different. Since there was neither current utility nor income from it, an owner may have defaulted on his taxes through no flaw in the land itself. Thus, a tax lien on vacant land can be a perfectly valid investment. The objective, of course, is to hold the land thus acquired until it has matured in value. Bearing in mind that the price you pay is usually well below the market value of the parcel, the risk is relatively small.

This does not mean that you should forego a thorough investigation of the area and its development potential before buying. In some cases, for instance, an owner may default on taxes and thereby abandon the property, primarily because, under existing zoning laws it does not lend itself to profitable development. If this is the case, it would not be a desirable investment.

Municipalities vary in their practices of tax foreclosure and lien sales. Let us assume, however, that three years of unpaid back taxes would bring about a tax sale. On a $50,000 piece of land that is assessed at about $16,000, at a $10 per $100 tax rate, one year's taxes are $1,600, and three years of taxes would amount to $4,800. In an auction, $4,800 would be the *upset price* and bidding would begin there. In a direct sale, the price would be $4,800 plus whatever costs the authorities ascribe to the foreclosure process. In all likelihood, this piece of land could be purchased for less

Land Investments **85**

than $10,000. The question of how much it would yield in a resale, either immediately or at a later date, depends entirely upon the reasons for the foreclosure. If there is a fatal flaw in the property, such as an inability to develop it, it may not be worth anywhere near $10,000. But if the foreclosure stemmed from an independent source of distress, such as the owner's bankruptcy or the bankruptcy of his business, the lien may be an excellent investment.

Chapter 8
Home Sites on the Installment Plan

For those of you not courageous or experienced enough to invest in vacant land individually, there are many offerings from land development companies. These fall into two general classes: in some areas, development companies offer home sites on the installment plan as part of a community building venture. Elsewhere, land is sold as an independent entity, giving the investor the choice of either building on it or merely holding it for future resale or for the construction of a home through his own contractor. Both approaches have certain advantages.

Installment sales of either type are different from ordinary land sales. Under both plans, the investor signs a contract to purchase one or more lots for a stated down payment and monthly installments until the full price plus interest is paid. Only when he has made his final payment does he receive the deed to his property. Until then, he has none of the tax advantages—such as the deductibility of his real estate taxes and mortgage interest when reporting his annual income—he would have if he bought a parcel on his own.

LAND DEVELOPMENT PROJECTS

The following is a typical case of an investment in a land development project. An investor is offered a lot in a new development at a stated price of

Home Sites on the Installment Plan **87**

$4,000. The arrangement calls for a down payment of $400 and subsequent payments of $50 a month for a period of six years. The developer's price of $4,000 includes the interest he is paying on the mortgage portion applicable to the investor's plot. It is the investor, therefore, who is paying the interest for the developer, but it is the latter who reaps the tax benefits from the deductible interest. In effect, the investor is paying interest on his installment package. This is not to be construed as unethical. Anything a consumer buys on the time-payment plan is interest-bearing. Moreover, the developer's prospectus is expected to spell this out clearly. The only disadvantage of buying land in this manner is that the investor does not receive the income tax benefits. To all intents and purposes, he is really buying a lot that cost the developer far less. If the land is worth $4,000, you, the investor, may have made a wise investment. And if the developer is reliable and successful, that lot should be worth more than $4,000 by the time you receive the deed as ultimate owner.

It is really on the fulfillment of the promise that the land will increase in value and in the prospects of growth in the developer's community, that the decision to invest finally lies. There are land developments under way in many attractive parts of the country, including Florida, Arizona, New Mexico and the Pocono Mountains section of Pennsylvania. Usually these areas are deemed attractive as retirement or vacation communities. Their recent history gives a clue to their growth as an investment vehicle.

RETIREMENT COMMUNITIES

Soon after World War II, Florida was rediscovered as a potential retirement haven. Several large corporations gained prominence through their plans to provide retirement housing on the installment plan. The original idea was to permit people still gainfully employed to set aside monthly sums from their incomes toward a piece of land on which to build a residence when they retired. The inducements were ample. A warm, pleasant climate; community facilities already standing. And, in some instances, developers even pointed to employment opportunities in the area for those who were not planning to spend their retirement years in a rocking chair. The corporations' success was almost instantaneous; perhaps too much so, because they were soon followed into the field by marginal operators whose communities could not utlimately provide what had been promised.

To make these land sales possible, a developer needed to create the nucleus of his community. This entailed at least one section of a new village that included attractive houses, power and sewer plant, recreational center, golf course, and a variety of facilities, including a town hall. Of course, the lots being sold for delivery some years hence did not have to be developed until later. Buyers would simply choose their parcels from maps, and this opened the door to some abuses.

For instance, some lots intended for future development might still be

88 *Real Estate for Active Investment*

under water. And, in some cases, a single lot selling at the low advertised price would not be sufficient for construction of a house, and the buyer would be forced to invest in two or three lots to make his purchase viable. Some of the worst offenders were those who showed customers drawings of the proposed golf course and clubhouse. But by the time the buyer had paid off most of his land, he would discover that no progress had been made on either the clubhouse, or the sewer and power plants, shopping center, and other promised amenities. In the worst instances, not even the land was ready to be built upon.

Happily, many of these abuses have been eradicated in most areas. In Florida, for example, the Florida Land Sales Commission was established to police land developers and make them adhere to accepted standards of selling and advertising. In addition, the attorneys general of many states require that land installment sales offerings, no matter where they are located, must pass muster before they can be offered for sale within that state. Furthermore, in some instances the Securities and Exchange Commission has claimed jurisdiction on the grounds that these were public offerings in the same sense as the public offerings of stocks and bonds.

Soon after the first retirement communities came on the market with land offerings, others followed with the idea of attracting younger families. The proffered attraction was an opportunity to resettle and begin a new career in a thriving new area. Subsequently, land developers have discovered that they don't need to offer anything besides the land itself, and advertise simply the advantage or owning one or several lots in an area with a potential for growth. As evidence, they construct either a resort or some commercial facilities around which a community can develop.

However, despite the surveillance by several legal authorities, the land development business has remained under a cloud in the minds of many. In fact, a major land development company has been indicted by the federal government for allegedly misrepresenting the value of its merchandise. This is due, primarily, to the promotional atmosphere in which land is sold. Since most of these developments are usually in relatively remote areas where raw land is inexpensive to the developer, the sale must be made on the prospective buyer's home ground. This means that he is first approached through telephone squads or at dinners arranged by local sales organizations; dinners at which first motion pictures of the community are shown and then the salesmen make their pitch over dessert and coffee. In some cases, a deposit on contract entitles the prospect to a free or cut-rate trip to the land development, where the sales force greets him to finalize the sale. Some of these contracts also stipulate that if the buyer should change his mind in midstream, he forfeits the payments made up to that point.

Citing these procedures should not be regarded as a condemnation. This is, perhaps, the only feasible way to launch a land development venture of this type. There are many thriving communities today whose birth took place in the above manner. Unfortunately, cases where things go awry

Home Sites on the Installment Plan   **89**

make headlines, just as the news from Hollywood has traditionally been dominated by divorces of movie stars, rather than by blissful marriages. The lesson to be learned, therefore, is that familiarity with an area is a *sine qua non* of a successful investment. If, indeed, an investor is inclined to buy land on the installment plan in Florida, Arizona, New Mexico, or the Poconos, he should first invest both the time and money needed to investigate the locale thoroughly.

Federal law has now liberalized the rescission rights of land buyers. As a result, most land companies offer investors the right to their money back if (a) they change their minds several days after they signed on the dotted line or (b) if they change their minds during a visit to the development site within six months of signing.

When an investor does combine vacation fun with a serious look at the prospects in various parts of the area, he will have a clearer understanding of where the real values lie. There is no doubt that there are developments in any of these sections of the country in which a lot, bought on installments, will be worth many times its original price. To verify the claims made by developers, an investor should discuss the offerings with independent local real estate brokers, bankers, and even some residents of the community in which he is considering a purchase. While nobody can eliminate the risks altogether, they can certainly be reduced through the same kind of precaution one would take in investing in land on an individual basis. Moreover, this method of checking out an offering may also uncover a better deal that the investor can make on his own.

Chapter 9
Industrial and Commercial Buildings

Let us pause for a moment to see where we have been and where we can still go in the world of small real estate investments. We are now acquainted with various methods of owning real estate for use as well as for investment, such as year-round homes, vacation residences, stores or offices. We have also looked into land investments for their own sake, and more specifically, at investments in vacant land. Yet, land is still a rather passive investment. It is much like merchandise bought for eventual resale at a profit, and it requires little effort on the part of the owner to make this resale viable. For the investor who wants to acquire some know-how in managing his property, we will now explore some areas that point out at least a few of the characteristics of an active real estate business. It is through this type of investment that one can acquire the skills which may, at a later date, enable the investor to devote much—or even all—of his time to real estate as his full occupation. These skills can be valuable for several reasons. Airline pilots, athletes, those with particularly strenuous physical occupations, or even those suddenly afflicted with an illness that may terminate their basic careers, can turn to real estate investments as a source of income to replace the wages or salaries they used to receive.

Real estate need not be an all-consuming activity from an investor's point of view. But as we become more steeped in it, there are details which need constant attention and surveillance. Let us begin, therefore, with a

Industrial and Commercial Buildings **91**

transition phase in which there is only a modicum of activity—the **leaseback.**

THE LEASEBACK

Until now, we have examined both properties which produce annual income, as well as land which is held essentially for profit upon resale. In both cases, it was the owner who was in daily charge of the property. Not so in a **leaseback.** This term is derived from a simpler concept, which is the **net lease.** Under a typical net lease, the tenant maintains the property, sometimes pays all of the taxes, interest and amortization on the mortgage, and, in addition, pays a rental to the owner of the building. This type of lease is used primarily for industrial and commercial buildings occupied by a single tenant, such as a manufacturing plant or a one-store retail property. Let us look at a simple example of how it works.

The typical property might be an industrial building containing 10,000 square feet of production space. Normally, a building of this kind contains an office area equivalent to about 10 percent of the total area. Most of the time, such buildings are occupied by small manufacturing concerns that are either owned independently or are a subsidiary of a larger corporation. In either case, those who manage the business use the 10 percent, or 1,000 square feet, for their offices. The remaining 9,000 square feet is open production area. For purposes of this discussion, we shall regard it as a 10,000-square-foot building.

The surrounding land, if there is any, is irrelevant to this examination. It is assumed that, in a modern industrial area, there is a parking lot and some landscaped space around the building. However, in terms of cost, the land plays a small role. Industrial parks are usually built in relatively undeveloped areas on the fringes of a city, where land is fairly inexpensive. If the industrial building is closer to midtown, there is probably little or no land included, but what there is sells at a higher price. The two locations, therefore, are more or less equivalent. For the sake of simplicity, let us assume that the 10,000-square-foot building, representing about one-quarter of an acre, stands on a one-half acre parcel (approximately 20,000 square feet).

Provided it is not already well developed and thriving with industry, land on the fringes of the city might be worth $10,000 a half-acre. An industrial building, which is essentially a shell made of steel and cinder blocks with a concrete floor, can be built for about $15 a square foot, since it contains no basement and provides few internal appurtenances. While the basic construction does provide heating and plumbing (including provision for washrooms), it is a very primitive affair, indeed. Electrical wiring is usually brought only as far as the perimeter of the building, since each manufacturer requires different circuitry for his particular operation. Heating is normally provided through air ducts, and, if air conditioning is included, the same ductwork is used, thus requiring only the compressor to

92 *Real Estate for Active Investment*

produce cooling. Office partitioning is installed by the occupant as, of course, are the fixtures required for the manufacturing process. It matters little, in this example, whether the original builder or the tenant provides the extras, such as office partitioning, washroom facilities or locker-room walls, because these are compensated for in the price of the original building.

At $15 a square foot, therefore, we have a building worth $150,000 on a $10,000 piece of land, for a total of $160,000. The financing of this sum becomes the prime consideration at this point.

FINANCING

Since industrial space is not rented as readily as, say, a three-room apartment, the ability to obtain a mortgage hinges on the reliability of the tenant. Before an institution, such as a bank, insurance company, or pension fund, makes a mortgage commitment, it wants to be certain that the tenant has a viable business, as well as the resources to pay his rent over the period of the lease. Moreover, the mortgage lender will be reluctant to provide a mortgage over a period that is longer than the underlying lease of the tenant. After all, that lease is virtually all the security he has, other than the financial resources of the building's owner. And as the owner of the building, the investor really does not want to risk more than his mortgage lender. Put another way, if the tenant defaults, the building no longer produces income until a new tenant is found. This means the owner, i.e., you, the investor, must either pay mortgage interest out of your own pocket or forfeit the property in foreclosure, unless you find a new tenant quickly.

INDUSTRIAL AND COMMERCIAL LEASES

Industrial and commercial leases, unlike those for apartments, are drawn for substantially longer terms. There are good reasons for this. As we said before, a landlord cannot replace an industrial tenant as readily as he can the departing occupant of a small apartment. It is in his best interest to have assurance that the tenant will stay for many years. The tenant, too, likes a fairly long-term lease. Unlike his counterpart in an apartment, he cannot just call in the moving van and relocate. He has a substantial investment, not only in the machinery which must be moved, but also in the installation of his equipment (the electric circuits and plumbing that feed the machinery and the intricate assembly lines which are part of many manufacturing processes). The engineering fees alone for designing a new plant facility can be staggering. As a result, industrial leases might have an initial term of ten years, and several renewal options of five or ten years each, sometimes aggregating twenty-five or more years.

There is another difference between apartment and industrial tenants. As we discussed in the case of the apartment, the landlord requires two months' extra rent at the outset of the rental to serve as security. If he is

Industrial and Commercial Buildings **93**

wise, he will also make a cursory check into his prospective tenant's ability to pay. These two precautions are usually sufficient. However, in preparing a commercial or industrial lease, the credit investigation is far more exhaustive. It includes a fairly thorough investigation into the tenant company's history, and into the history of the industry within which he operates. If he is making buggy whips, forget it, because the business won't last.

As for the tenant's ability to meet his rent and other obligations, the property owner would be inexcusably negligent if he did not obtain a financial reference from Dun & Bradstreet, or an even more private report from such credit searchers as Bishop's Reports.* If the prospective tenant is a subsidiary owned by another, larger concern, the landlord may require a guarantee from the parent company to pay the obligations for the actual tenant, should he default.

THE MORTGAGE

Having secured a tenant who meets these financial requirements, the owner of a new industrial building can begin negotiating with a bank or insurance company for a mortgage. Let us say, therefore, that he finds a backer who will provide a mortgage for two-thirds of the property's value of $160,000, or $106,000. Such a mortgage might, under current conditions, call for interest of 10 percent. As we discovered in our example of a store building, such mortgages are usually structured to require constant payments which include interest as well as some amortization. The constant payment, in this instance, might be 12 percent a year, or about $12,720. As for the owner of the building, he must make a cash down payment of $54,000, which is probably more than he cares to invest. He can, therefore, take on a second mortgage of $30,000, and pay only $24,000 in cash. As we found earlier, a second mortgage might have an interest rate of 15 percent because of the inherently higher risk. This means annual interest payments of $4,500. The second mortgage in this example is a **standing mortgage** for five years and requires no amortization payments.

THE ECONOMICS

Just to carry the building's financing, then, the owner must pay a total of $17,220, not counting taxes and all of the other costs of owning an industrial building, including insurance, heating, and maintenance. It becomes quickly apparent that a manufacturer could be his own landlord and face approximately the same annual carrying charges. But to him, the landlord's initial investment in the building of even $24,000 represents

---

*Dun & Bradstreet, Inc., is perhaps the best known of credit reporting agencies. Bishop's Reports, another firm of this type, is frequently used for more investigative reports into a subject's financial condition.

94 *Real Estate for Active Investment*

costs of machines and raw materials, essential to the business. He is therefore better off letting someone else buy the building and instead paying rent to a landlord. Also, from the manufacturer's point of view, there are tax advantages in being a tenant rather than an owner.

As we found in our examination of a building with retail stores or offices, the owner works with a budget which includes not only the interest and amortization on the mortgages, but also the insurances, heating, and maintenance. It is here that the net lease begins to make sense from the investor's point of view.

THE BUDGET

Let us take a look at comparative budgets for just the first five years. Here is what the building's owner pays annually:

Constant payment of 12% (including 10% interest and 2% amortization on 1st mortgage of $106,000)	$12,720
Interest of 15% on 2nd mortgage of $30,000	4,500
Taxes (based upon 50% assessment, or $80,000 valuation, with tax rate of $10 per $100 of valuation)	8,000
Insurance (on building only)	5,000
Maintenance	3,000
Total annual costs	$33,220
If the owner of that building wants to earn a 12% yield on his investment of $24,000, this would be	2,880
Annual reserve for retirement of 2nd mortgage	6,000
Rent he must therefore charge his tenant per year (or $4.21 per square foot)	$42,100

One thing becomes apparent from this. The owner's insurance costs on the building alone are relatively low. After all, the building itself is just a shell of steel and concrete or cinder blocks. The real value which must be adequately insured lies in the equipment and furnishings inside that belong to the tenant. Also, there is little maintenance cost to the owner of the building. An industrial building requires relatively little maintenance, since most of the chores of day-to-day upkeep are more related to the manufacturing process than they are to the building itself. Most manufacturers, even of relatively small size, will therefore keep a maintenance man on their regular payrolls.

Since the combining of the insurance on the building with the interior coverage of equipment and furnishings usually results in a somewhat smaller premium, there are possible savings for the tenant if he assumes responsibility for insurance and maintenance. By the same token, utilizing the manufacturer's maintenance man for chores pertaining to work on the basic building should produce some worthwhile economizing for the

Industrial and Commercial Buildings **95**

investor. It makes sense, therefore, to draw a lease under which these two items are to be paid by the tenant and under which the annual rent reflects this transferral of responsibility. In real estate parlance, this is known as a **net lease.** In terms of rent payments, it simply means that the landlord, or investor, requires only $30,220 a year to earn his yield of 12 percent.

THE NET, NET LEASE

Even more popular is the so-called **net, net lease.** Under this concept, the tenant assumes all of the charges, including the following:

Constant payment for interest and amortization on 1st mortgage of $106,000	$12,720
Interest on 2nd mortgage of $30,000	4,500
Taxes	8,000
Insurance and maintenance at whatever cost	—
Rent to owner of building	8,880
(This gives the owner a 12% yield on $24,000 investment plus reserve to repay 2nd mortgage at five years)	*(or 89¢ per square foot)*

From the investor's point of view, this is a very satisfactory arrangement. Not only does he receive his 12 percent return on investment, but he also benefits from the depreciation of the building. If the $150,000 building is deemed to have a useful life of fifty years (remember, the $10,000 piece of land does not depreciate) he can deduct 2 percent, or $3,000, from his taxable income.

If there is one flaw in this arrangement, it is the problem of how the investor will repay the unamortized balance of the first mortgage at the end of ten years. At that point, with 2 percent of annual amortization taken from the constant payments, the original $106,000 first mortgage will have been reduced to a **balloon** of $84,800. If the tenant's lease expires at the same time as the mortgage, it might be difficult for the investor to replace the first mortgage with a new loan unless the tenant has already exercised his option for at least another five years of occupancy. One easy remedy is to get the tenant to sign an original **net, net lease** with an initial term of fifteen or twenty years.

Once the second mortgage has been paid off, the $6,000 reserve can be applied to the reduction of the first mortgage. At the end of ten years, then, $30,000 is available for the repayment of the expiring first mortgage. The **balloon,** however, is $84,800. This means that the investor should shop for a new first mortgage of $54,800, which, with a 12 percent constant payment, should not be hard to get. For the second ten years, the budget will look like this:

96 *Real Estate for Active Investment*

The tenant pays:	
Constant payment of 12% for interest and amortization on new 1st mortgage of $54,800	$6,576
Taxes	8,000
Insurance and maintenance at whatever cost	—
Rent to owner of building	8,360 (or 84¢ per square foot)
This continues to give owner a 12% yield on $24,000 invest- ment	2,880
Plus reserve to repay 1st mortgage in 10 years	5,480

In actual practice, however, it does not work exactly this way. First of all, the tenant cannot take the risk at the outset of his rental of not knowing what kind of mortgage will replace the first mortgage when it expires. Nor does the investor wish to limit his yield to 12 percent forever. The simple solution, therefore, is to figure backwards. If, throughout the twenty-year lease, the tenant budgets an average of $4.00 a square foot, he knows that, on the average, it will cost him $40,000 a year to occupy the 10,000-square-foot premises. He will pay, say, $9,000 of this a year to the investing owner, which should always cover his yield and reserve against mortgage maturities. With the remainder he will meet his obligations under a net, net lease for mortgage interest, taxes, insurance, and maintenance. In return, his lease agreement will limit the amount of mortgage interest he will have to pay in any one year, in case the owner tries to burden the property with an excessively large mortgage. As a rule, the original mortgage is known at the time the lease is made, and a fairly accurate determination of the refinancing can be made well in advance.

As the investor's need for reserves against mortgage maturities diminish, his yield from the investment rises. Under some net, net leases, the tenant's net rent—what he pays directly to the landlord—may also increase periodically under the lease, reflecting the changing conditions in the economy during the long-term period of the arrangement.

Let's look at it another way. At an annual yield of even 12 percent, or $2,880, the investor will recapture his original investment of $24,000 after eight years and four months; and even sooner if he takes into account his income tax savings from the depreciation. Since the tenant's lease extends well beyond that magical date, there is little risk that the investor will not, at the very least, get his money back, and this *is* a very important consideration. In this context, it should be pointed out that industrial and commercial leases, made with responsible tenants, represent a lesser risk than a lease with an apartment tenant. There is little point in pursuing an apartment tenant who skips out in the dead of night, considering the possible cost of the chase. With industrial or commercial tenants, there is seldom such a chase. If the proper credit investigations are made in advance, or if a

Industrial and Commercial Buildings **97**

third party, such as the parent corporation, has guaranteed the rent payments, there should be no fear of a tenant's sudden departure. The mere impossibility of a sudden dismantling of an industrial operation would militate against it.

The only real threat would be the unexpected bankruptcy of the tenant. If the tenant decides to move out for understandable reasons, such as the need to relocate his production for business reasons, he remains responsible for the rent and therefore must pay it even if the space is empty. Or, he must provide a sublessee for the remainder of his contractual lease term. To protect himself against unexpected bankruptcy, the landlord normally requires, in his lease terms, that the tenant furnish him with audited financial statements. From these statements, the owner of the building can usually discern at an early stage that the tenant is running into trouble. Armed with this knowledge, the landlord can discuss the matter candidly with the tenant and, if necessary, begin to notify real estate brokers to cast about for another tenant in the event the building becomes vacant. Furthermore, the landlord is in a preferred position in that he can lock up the building and take possession of the machinery. In most states, under real estate law, any asset permanently affixed to the real estate reverts to the owner of the fee (basic real estate or the building) unless otherwise stipulated in a lease.

A **net lease,** or **net, net lease,** therefore, provides an investor not only with a source of income, but also introduces him to some of the active work of owning real estate for investment. Net leases require a modicum of continuous involvement with the property on the part of the investor, an involvement which can be of great value later in his career as a realty man.

Let us not forget that this discussion began with the examination of a leaseback. How does it differ from the net, net lease we have just described? Until now, we predicated this discussion on an example whereby a new building was created by the investor. The chances are small, however, that he would undertake this complex project as a novice in the field. No doubt, there are relatively new industrial buildings for sale in which he can invest, once a tenant has been signed for a net lease. But the prospects of such an investment are even better in situations where the manufacturer presently owns his own building.

Leasebacks have their greatest appeal to manufacturing companies which originally built or bought their own plants. Many of these manufacturers discover that it is sometimes advantageous to generate cash for a specific business purpose, such as new equipment, for example. They can borrow the money on a short-term basis, but the chances are that they have already borrowed all their bank will allow. They could increase the mortgage on their plant, but there is a question of whether the property can bear additional mortgage credit. So it makes sense for such manufacturers to generate the cash by selling the plant and leasing it back from the new owner. This creates another investment opportunity for those inclined to buy real estate.

98 *Real Estate for Active Investment*

Once more, using the example of the $160,000 plant, it is easy to see why it would make sense to buy it from the manufacturer for $24,000 and make a net, net lease with him. In all likelihood, however, $24,000 is not enough to meet his needs for quick cash; $50,000 would be more like it. To the investor, this means buying the property for $210,000, or $50,000 more than he did in the previous example. For the manufacturer, it would have the following consequences:

1. If he had the same mortgages as described in the previous example, he owes $106,000 on the first mortgage (minus any amortization already paid) and $30,000 on the second mortgage.

2. Since he owns the building, he is now paying all of the annual charges outlined before, except that he pays no rent to the landlord.

3. To sell the property to an investor and lease it back, he can either elect to repay the outstanding mortgages and let the new owner obtain his own loans, or he can assign the mortgages to the new owner—the investor—provided, of course, the mortgage agreement gives him the right to make such an assignment. Under an assignment, the purchaser of a property simply assumes the mortgage obligations of the seller.

Now let us look at the investor's consequences. If he buys the property for $210,000 and assumes the existing mortgages totaling $136,000, he must produce a cash down payment of $74,000. This is obviously more than the middle-income investor can afford. Therefore, he must look to entirely new mortgage financing to make the deal.

Since the value of the property has been established at $210,000, by virtue of an actual sale, and since there is an incumbent tenant to pay the rent required under a long-term net, net lease, a mortgage lender should have little hesitation in granting a first mortgage for two-thirds of that value, or $140,000. Once again, let us make it a ten-year mortgage at 12 percent constant payments. This leaves $70,000 to be paid, of which $40,000 can probably be obtained in the form of a second mortgage. This would be a five-year loan at 15 percent interest. The investor, in this case, would look for a 12 percent return on his $30,000, or $3,600 a year plus, once again, the tax benefits of depreciation. To make this feasible, the manufacturer, now a tenant in a $210,000 property, must adhere to this budget for the first five years, as shown in top table on page 99.

What does this mean to the manufacturer-turned-tenant? As the owner of the property, then valued at $160,000, what he paid annually for the first five years is shown in bottom table on page 99.

Since the manufacturer would pay taxes, insurance, and maintenance in any event, whether he owns or net, net leases the building, the difference in financing costs between owning and leasing the property is $12,180 a year for the first five years, or $60,900. After that, the interest of $6,000 and

Industrial and Commercial Buildings **99**

Rent (to yield owner 12% return on $30,000)	$ 3,600
Constant 12% payment on 1st mortgage of $140,000	16,800
Interest of 15% on 2nd mortgage of $40,000	6,000
Reserve to retire 2nd mortgage at 5 years	8,000
Reserve to amortize unpaid principal of 1st mortgage at 10 years, considering that constant payment includes 2% amortization (1st mortgage will be down to $112,000)	6,000
Total cost to tenant	$40,400

Constant payment on 1st mortgage of $106,000	$12,720
Interest on 2nd mortgage of $30,000	4,500
Reserve to retire 2nd mortgage at 5 years	6,000
Reserve to reduce 1st mortgage to $34,800 at 10 years	5,000
Total financing costs (per year)	$28,220

reserve of $8,000 on the second mortgage fall away. His annual finance charges plus rent for the second five years are reduced to $26,400, or $1,820 less than they were when he owned the building. In effect, he can look upon his net proceeds of $50,000 from the sale of the building as a five-year loan which he repaid in the sum of $60,900. The difference of $10,900 could be considered interest at the rate of $2,180 a year, or 4.3 percent. Where else could he have borrowed $50,000 at 4.3 percent—if he could have borrowed it at all?

For the real estate investor, the purchase of the building provided an annual return of 12 percent in addition to the tax benefit of the building's depreciation. Once again, the original investment of $30,000 was recaptured in eight years and four months, or less if he includes the income tax savings.

To sweeten the pot for himself, the investor could also have drawn a lease under which the tenant's rent of $3,600 a year increases after the first five years. This is certainly fair when one considers the extremely low cost of having used the $50,000 for five years. Let us just say that after the first five years of the lease, the tenant raises the rent to $4,500, yielding the investor 15 percent. He should have little trouble doing this, because the tenant's financing charges dropped by $1,400 when the second mortgage matured. Comes the end of ten years, the tenant's obligations on the first mortgage also decrease materially, justifying a further rise in rent for the benefit of the investor.

As in any investment, there are cautions which should be kept in mind with a leaseback. While the tenant is responsible for interest and amortization payments on the first and second mortgages, the lien against the property—the legal claim inherent in a mortgage—remains the responsibility of the owner. If the tenant fails to make any of the required payments, it is the owner who will be notified by the lending institution. But by this

100 *Real Estate for Active Investment*

time it may be too late. The tenant may already be in serious financial trouble. This is why it is doubly important to keep constant track of the tenant's financial condition by demanding audited statements annually or even quarterly. Of course, considering that the investor receives, in addition to his basic yield, the reserve payments for the retirement of the mortgages, a serious delinquency would rear its head in sufficient time. In the leaseback example shown here, the total reserves amount to $14,000 a year, or $3,500 quarterly. In effect, the investor collects a total of $4,400 quarterly, including his return on investment, a sum which should arrive in the mail at the appointed dates. If one of these payments is late, it is an indication that something is amiss.

Leasebacks, as stated earlier, are generally workable when a single tenant occupies the property. This might not only be an industrial enterprise, but also a building containing a department or specialty store occupying the entire space. There are more complex versions of the leaseback, in which the leaseback tenant is a real estate entrepreneur in his own right, who in turn rents the property out to several tenants. In such cases, of course, this intermediary must also have a profit motive. As a result, rents in such a building would run slightly higher to enable the investor to reap his yield of, say, 12 percent and allow for a middle man's profit besides.

Chapter 10
Leaseholds

From a small investor's point of view, the middle man's position is an interesting one as well. In this guise he takes on an identity which resembles that of both the landlord and the tenant. It provides him with another form of leverage, that all-important concept in real estate. Since he does not have to buy a building, his investment may be smaller. But, on the other side of the coin, he can pass many of his costs along to the property's tenants. Admittedly, the leasehold position is somewhat more complex, because it does involve more constant daily attention to the property. However, it is worth a brief discussion at this point.

FEE OWNERSHIP

To understand the leasehold, we should first come to grips with some basic concepts of real estate ownership not previously examined. The most elementary of these is known as **fee ownership.** Simply stated, it is the outright title to a piece of land with a building on it. Also known as "fee simple," it means that the owner has unimpeded right and title to the land and any improvements which may either be on it or which he may wish to erect on it. Normally, these are the terms under which a family owns its home. Fee ownership may be owned by an individual or by two or more

102 *Real Estate for Active Investment*

people, such as a man and his wife. It may be owned by a partnership, corporation, trust, or other types of associations.

THE LEASEHOLD

Another form of ownership to be discussed here is the **leasehold.** As the name implies, the owner of a leasehold leases, or rents, the land from the owner of the fee for an agreed price known as *ground rent*. Like any lease, it calls for rental payments and has a finite term. During that term, the owner of the leasehold has certain privileges regarding the use or disposition of the grounds that are spelled out in the leasehold agreement itself. However, at no time does the fee owner part with his ultimate and perpetual right to the property until he sells it. It is somewhat akin to the idea of a man owning a tree and giving someone else the right to pick and sell the fruit from the tree for a stipulated period of time. Throughout this time, the original owner retains possession of the tree. And when the term of the lease expires, even the fruit crops on the tree again belong to the owner. In a real estate leasehold, whatever is permanently affixed to the land reverts to the owner of the land, or fee. As we explained in an earlier example, any permanent improvement that is a part of the property reverts to the owner when the lease is ended.

Because of the economics of leaseholds—the cost of erecting a building, for instance—such agreements are usually written for longer terms than, say, an apartment lease. It would not make sense to build an apartment house on land owned by somebody else, only to give up all rights to the building two years later. In most instances, a leasehold agreement provides for an initial term of several years, with stated options for renewal every few years thereafter (usually for a maximum of ninety-nine years). This may seem to be an arbitrary limit, but there is a good reason for it.

Historically, possession of a property for a hundred years or more has been viewed as tantamount to full ownership of it. And since there are certain tax advantages in having a leasehold, the agreement should avoid any provisions which could be construed to be actual ownership or a subterfuge for it. We will examine the tax implications at a later point.

Creating a leasehold, therefore, is to split a property into two components. One is the land itself, and the other is the building on it. In another form of leasehold, the split may be along somewhat different lines. The fee may consist of both the land and the building, while the leasehold position merely gives the lessee, or tenant, the right to operate it. One can readily see how there may be even a three-way split in this concept: the first party owns the land, the second leases the land and erects a building on it, and a third party leases the right to operate the building. With each split in the line of ownership, additional leverage is created. We examined the role of the lever earlier. It proved that one can lift a heavy object easily by pushing down on the other end of the lever. Now consider the leverage of a leasehold.

LEASEHOLD LEVERAGE

The leasehold makes it feasible for an investor to reap the profits of owning a building for a period of time without buying it. Obviously, the greatest benefits of investing in a leasehold can be derived when the land represents a major portion of the overall cost of the property. If the land were worth very little compared with the total value of the property, the investor might as well purchase the property outright. However, if being spared the land purchase reduces the price of the building materially, the difference becomes readily apparent, as shown in the following paragraph.

Let us consider the building with four stores analyzed in the previous chapter. It made sense to purchase it outright for $156,000, subject to mortgages. After all, the land represented only $12,000 of the total value. Move this property to the best shopping location in a city, and the picture changes considerably. The land might well be worth five times as much, or about $60,000. The total property, then, would be worth in excess of $200,000. As a result, taxes would be higher, but so would the rents charged to the stores' tenants. There is a position, now, for a middle man. Let's see how it works.

THE MIDDLE MAN

We are now looking at a downtown store property, near what is known as the "100 percent location," or the best shopping corner in town. The property consists of a 7,200-square-foot piece of land, sixty feet deep, with 120 feet of street frontage. As in the earlier example, the land is improved with the addition of a building of the same size which houses four stores, each sixty feet deep, with thirty feet of street frontage. Considering its prime location, the land has a market value of $60,000. The building has a market value of $144,000, based upon a construction cost of $20 a square foot. On this premise, the total value of the property is $204,000. It is owned by Mr. X, in his own right a real estate investor. The chances are that he also has a mortgage on the property, but this plays no role in our example, since with the creation of his leasehold, he will probably pay it off. As we will see later, it makes more sense for him to sell the leasehold than to maintain the mortgage or mortgages on his land and building.

THE INVESTOR

Enter the investor. He is not in a position to buy a $204,000 property, but he can invest up to $35,000. Upon negotiation with Mr. X, he agrees to buy the leasehold for half the property's market value, or $102,000. Why can he buy it so cheaply? And why does Mr. X agree to sell it for that price? First, the investor is not really buying the entire property at all. He is merely buying the right to use the building as its temporary owner for a given number of years. When the term of his leasehold expires, the building returns to the

104 *Real Estate for Active Investment*

ownership of Mr. X. In addition, the investor pays Mr. X an annual rent for the land and building and undertakes to carry all of the costs of financing and maintaining the building during the interim. In effect, all of the ground rent the investor pays Mr. X is clear income to Mr. X, much like the net, net lease we discussed before.

LEASEHOLD MORTGAGES

Still, $102,000 is more cash than the investor has available. He can therefore go to a mortgage-lending institution and apply for a so-called **leasehold mortgage.** Such a mortgage differs little from an ordinary mortgage on a property owned in fee. The primary difference lies in the collateral. An ordinary mortgage on a fee provides that, in the event of the owner's default on mortgage payments for interest or amortization, the lender can foreclose and thereby repossess the entire property, land and building. The lender of a leasehold mortgage has no lien against the land at all. Should he need to foreclose, he can gain possession of only one thing—the right to operate the building as did the investor to whom he granted the mortgage. As we can see, there is a definite value attached to that right, as represented in a leasehold agreement.

In this instance, let us say that the investor can obtain a leasehold mortgage for two-thirds of the $102,000 value of the leasehold, or $68,000. This leaves a cash investment of $34,000, or just about what the investor intended to spend.

Because the lender cannot gain control of the fee itself, his risk is somewhat greater than it would be in an ordinary first mortgage. Hence, he will probably demand a higher interest rate of, let us say, 12 percent a year. He will also seek some amortization, of perhaps, 2 percent, resulting in constant annual payments of 14 percent.

The term of the leasehold mortgage cannot possibly exceed the initial term of the leasehold, either. Should the investor choose not to exercise his options, the leasehold disappears from the face of the earth and with it the lender's only collateral.

Let us, then, assume that the initial term of the lease is ten years, and so is the term of the leasehold mortgage. Later we shall also examine the reasons for the relatively short initial term of leaseholds as part of the income tax implications of this investment.

Back to the property itself. We have established that it is near the best shopping location in town, and its market value reflects it. It is therefore assessed for real estate taxes at 50 percent of its value, or $102,000 (the tax assessor looks only at the value of the total property of $204,000, caring little about the fact that a leasehold exists). At a tax rate of $15 per $100 of assessed valuation, the real estate taxes on this property come to $15,300. Because of the property's excellent location, the space in the stores is also worth more money. Instead of $6 to $7 a square foot, as in the earlier example, merchants in this building will probably pay rent of $8 a square foot per year.

Leaseholds **105**

Let us now take another look at Mr. X., the fee owner, and his situation. He sold a leasehold on his $204,000 property for $102,000. This leaves him with his own investment of $102,000 in the land and building, on which he is entitled to a return of 12 percent. This takes the form of ground rent of $12,240 a year. It matters little whether Mr. X owns the land outright or not. His original mortgages on the property must be repaid when he creates the leasehold. After all, they were predicated on the fact that the entire property, land and building, served as collateral. Now he is giving up his rights to the building for at least ten years. The loan therefore is no longer valid, since his mortgage lender cannot possibly hold a lien against something the borrower has sold. Moreover, the investor would be foolish to purchase a leasehold on a building against which a prior lien exists. There are, of course, exotic ways of assigning Mr. X's original mortgage to the leasehold, but these would complicate our discussion. Let us just assume that Mr. X continues to own his property free and clear of mortgages, or that, following creation of the leasehold, he obtains a small mortgage on the land itself. It hardly concerns the investor.

THE ECONOMICS

From the investor's point of view, let us take a look at his annual budget for the property. The following are his principal expenses:

Ground rent	**$12,240**
Constant 14% payment for interest and amortization on leasehold mortgage of $68,000	9,520
Taxes ($15 per $100 on $102,000 valuation)	15,300
Heat and utilities	3,600
Maintenance and provision for vacancies	7,000
Total expenses	$47,660
He takes in rent ($8 per square foot on 7,200 square feet)	$57,600
This leaves him annually with	$ 9,940

Of this, he must set aside enough each year to retire the leasehold mortgage when it comes due after ten years. He cannot count on refinancing the **balloon,** because he cannot be sure that he will exercise his option for the next term. If he does not, he is stuck with the remaining principal on the leasehold mortgage. After ten years, that balloon will amount to $54,400, since he paid off 2 percent, or $1,360, as part of his 14 percent constant annual payments. After ten years, this comes to $13,600, thus reducing the original $68,000 leasehold mortgage to $54,400.

Of his $9,940 basic annual income, then, he sets aside $5,440 each year toward retirement of the leasehold mortgage. This leaves him with a net profit of $4,500, or a yield of 13.2 percent on his investment of $34,000.

This is not all, however. As the owner of a leasehold, an investor can enjoy tax advantages similar to those of depreciation, as described earlier. In this instance, though, the investor cannot depreciate the building, since

106 *Real Estate for Active Investment*

he does not own it. Still, when the leasehold expires, he literally has no tangible asset left, since the building reverts to Mr. X, the owner of the fee. He can therefore depreciate his investment in much the same way toward the day he gives up his rights in the building. Only in this case, rather than depreciation, it is properly called **leasehold amortization.**

How much amortization can he take each year? The Internal Revenue Service recognizes the possibility that the investor may not exercise his future options and that, as a result, he must cover the entire amortization during the initial term. In this example, it is ten years. Having paid $102,000 for the leasehold, he can take $10,200 each of these ten years as amortization. In the eyes of the tax authorities, he is losing $10,200 every year by the "wasting away" of his asset. In a tax sense, therefore, he is losing more ($10,200) than he is earning ($4,500). His "bottom line," the end result is a loss of $5,700 for tax purposes.

THE TAX SHELTER

The effect of this is known as a *tax shelter*. Not only is his yield of $4,500 a year sheltered against taxes—he pays no income tax on it—but he can apply the remaining loss of $1,200 against other income he may have. If, for example, his taxable income from his salary, after all other allowable deductions, is $30,000, he pays income taxes on only $28,800 of it. The benefit of tax sheltering varies according to each investor's income. If an investor's overall income is particularly large, he may be satisfied to purchase a leasehold or another real estate asset for its tax shelter alone. Such a person cares little about the actual return on investment. It is worth the effort just to be able to shelter a major part of his income by producing a loss such as we have shown here.

On the other hand, one cannot become too greedy. You may ask why the initial term of a leasehold is not two or three years instead of ten. The rate of leasehold amortization would be proportionately larger and therefore produce an even greater "loss" or tax shelter. Uncle Sam thought of this, too. The tax authorities' answer to this ploy is that an initial term of only two or three years is simply not believable since it would inevitably be a disastrous business deal, and was probably contrived merely to thwart the tax law. In such a case, the Internal Revenue Service would disallow such amortization and require that it be spread over ten or more years of the investor's option period.

Without being greedy, a leasehold is an excellent way to attain leverage. It actually enables two investors to reap income from the same property. Mr. X had a yield of 12 percent on his stake in the land and building. And the investor had a yield of 13.2 percent during the first ten years. In fact, Mr. X's return may have been somewhat greater. First, he might have obtained a mortgage on the land alone at an interest rate of less than 12 percent. Thus he gained some leverage by earning more than 12 percent on the total. If, for example, he had a $30,000 mortgage on his $60,000 parcel of land at 9 percent interest, his total yield would have been 12 percent on $72,000 of it less 9 percent on the mortgaged $30,000. Put it another way. His ground rent of $12,240 less $2,700 interest on the land mortgage, or $9,540, represents an annual yield of 13.2 percent on the $72,000 equity he had in the deal after the $30,000 mortgage on the land.

This is not all. Remember that, at the end of the final option term, the building reverts to the owner of the fee. Throughout this entire period, the building has been the fee owner's property, and he therefore retains the right to depreciate it, quite apart from the investor's leasehold amortization. If the building was worth $144,000 and deemed to have a useful life of fifty years, this means it has a 2 percent annual depreciation. This is a tax shelter of $2,880 for Mr. X as well. Stated another way, of the ground rent of $12,240 he received each year, only $9,360 was taxable income. In this connection, however, we must come back to the earlier point that the leasehold, including the initial term plus the renewal options, should not exceed a total of ninety-nine years. Were they longer, the tax authorities might consider the transaction an actual sale. In that case, Mr. X could not take depreciation on the building since, in effect, he sold it. Nor could the investor enjoy the tax shelter of leasehold amortization, as he would be regarded as the building's owner. As such, he could take the much smaller depreciation of 2 percent.

It is noteworthy, too, that both positions—the investor's leasehold and Mr. X's fee—are salable throughout the life of the leasehold. If Mr. X sold his fee ownership, his successor would simply start collecting the ground rent. He would be secure in the knowledge that a responsible lessee is obligated to pay a 12 percent yield no matter what happens, or he would have to give up the building to the new owner. As for the investor, he can sell his leasehold to someone else who finds it attractive. In fact, the next investor in the leasehold may be someone who will pay a high price for it if his only objective is the tax shelter inherent in that position. Of course, much depends upon the continuing viability of the retail business of the downtown area. If the neighborhood deteriorates, neither the fee owner nor the leasehold investor can escape the financial losses. If stores become vacant for long periods of time, the leaseholder, properly called **lessee,** will have trouble carrying the building and paying ground rent to Mr. X.

In this case, one of two things can happen. If the lessee defaults on his leasehold mortgage, the lending institution will foreclose and take over the leasehold. More than likely, the lender will also have trouble making the building pay and eventually approach the fee owner for a deal. If the investor, or lessee, defaults on his ground rent first, Mr. X will take the building away from him and try to run it himself. But first he must satisfy the leasehold mortgage since the collateral has been destroyed by termination of the leasehold. But Mr. X would have equally bad fortune operating the property in a blighted area. Unable to secure a sizable mortgage for it, he would probably be forced to offer it for a distress sale, i.e., sell it for a depressed price.

108 *Real Estate for Active Investment*

Obviously, everything depends upon the viability of the retail area, or the area in which any leasehold is located. This requires considerable understanding of the future prospects, best gained by a thorough acquaintance with the area to which the investor is planning to commit his funds. It also means a careful engineering study of the building itself to make certain that it requires no unforeseen major repairs or improvements, including those required to eliminate violations of the local building code. For an assessment of what the area holds in store, an investor should consult with local banks, the Chamber of Commerce, real estate brokers, and some of the merchants themselves. As for the physical condition of any building, regardless of whether it is a fee or leasehold investment, an engineer's study is well worth the price compared with the price one pays for the traumatic experience of having purchased an ailing structure.

RENEWAL OPTIONS

If an investor sees a downturn in neighborhood conditions or a serious physical defect arising in the structure of his building, he may choose not to exercise his renewal option after the first term or at any of the renewal periods. Incidentally, this is a good reason for structuring a leasehold to consist of an initial term and renewal options. The investor may well have had the ten or fifteen best years the property had to offer. Moreover, any costly improvements he makes in the building ultimately benefit Mr. X, to whom it eventually returns.

INFLATION

Another reason for renewal options is entirely financial. The amount of ground rent is in direct relationship to the market value of the property, both in terms of resale potential and income potential. Inflation plays a role in this. Assuming an inflation rate of only 5 percent a year, the $204,000 property should have a monetary value of $306,000 ten years hence. If the downtown area continues to thrive, it might well be worth nearly $400,000. This will also be reflected in the rents the merchants pay, as well as in property taxes, heating, utilities, and other maintenance items. Everything considered, however, the investor in a leasehold should expect increased income from the property as the years go by.

After ten years when he no longer needs to pay the $9,520 annually on the leasehold mortgage, his return will, indeed, be considerably greater. Mr. X knows this, too. He knows also that his property, now worth well over $300,000, would give him a far better return if he operated it as the fee owner. At the time the leasehold is created, therefore, Mr. X will insist that the ground rent reflect the same ratio to current value during each renewal term as it did during the initial period. In the example used here, the ground rent of $12,240 represented 6 percent of the property's total value of $204,000. Therefore, Mr. X will require that, upon renewal, the ground rent

Leaseholds **109**

for the next five years represent 6 percent of the property's value once more. The agreement usually stipulates that an appraisal be made at that point. If, after ten years, the property is appraised by an independent appraiser at $360,000, the ground rent automatically increases to 6 percent of this, or $21,600. The leasehold investor then must make the choice of renewing or not. If his store rents have increased proportionately, and if this provides him with a sufficient return after the increased realty taxes and other costs, he will be inclined to renew. If his yield drops to an unsatisfactory level, he should decline the option. In making this calculation, the investor must consider three factors:

1. He has now retired the leasehold mortgage and no longer needs to pay either the interest and amortization of $9,520 a year on it or hold the $5,440 reserve toward its repayment.
2. His tax shelter has also disappeared since he amortized the leasehold over the initial ten-year term.
3. He must look carefully at each of his store leases to determine whether they will carry him through the next five years without serious threat of vacancies. Not only must he check the number of remaining years in each of his tenants' leases, but he must consider whether their retail businesses are likely to endure. As in the net lease example studied earlier, he should always be aware of his tenants' financial status to protect himself against sudden closings or move-outs with the resultant defaults on leases.

This process repeats itself each time the leasehold comes up for another renewal option. Once we are past the first renewal, of course, the questions of leasehold mortgage and tax shelter are no longer operable. It should be pointed out, however, that an investor can always obtain a new leasehold mortgage during any term of his operation if he wishes to raise some cash. However, the payments on the new leasehold mortgage must be figured into his budget as part of his carrying charges, along with ground rent, taxes, and maintenance.

In describing the investment potential of leaseholds, we have actually delineated two investment possibilities. Not only did we learn about the leasehold itself, but we also took a look at the opportunities of playing the role of Mr. X, the fee owner. Endowed with somewhat more cash than our original investor, Mr. X has also made a wise investment. His function, of course, is considerably more passive. He need only sit there and collect the ground rent. It is much like the position of the investor in a net, net leaseback.

The investor in a leasehold is a far busier person. He must actually operate the building. Though we will spend some time later with the problems of actively operating a property, we must recognize at this point that being an active landlord, through a fee or leasehold, requires continu-

110 *Real Estate for Active Investment*

ous attention to many details. In larger properties, it may be worthwhile retaining a professional manager. But for a building containing only four stores, this should not be necessary. It can be accomplished along with an investor's regular obligations as a salary earner or professional.

Nor need we limit ourselves to a retail building. A leasehold can be created for virtually any type of real estate, be it an apartment house, hotel or motel, office building, or industrial structure. It is simply the middle position between a fee owner and a group of tenants. And as such, it can be very rewarding.

Chapter 11

Operating an Income Property

Like a tiger stalking its prey, we have walked around all sides of residential and commercial real estate to consider its various aspects. We have examined them in light of how they can provide us with extra income, and we have come to grips with leasing methods which, for a limited time at least, make us operators of such properties. Let us now become somewhat more detached and move in on the actual ownership of various types of income-producing real estate and perhaps find some ways in which we can make such investments directly.

To gain a valid understanding of such ventures, we must now study at closer range the challenges and problems of owning income properties. Until now, we have worked under the assumption that the potential investor knows generally how to acquire a property, how to operate it once he has purchased it, and even how to sell it profitably. To suggest that this knowledge is inbred into the human race is foolish. Therefore, let us acquaint ourselves with the basic principles.

SELECTING THE PROPERTY

As we have already determined, an income-producing property is one in which the occupants pay rents to the owner—rents that exceed the costs of operating the property, or repaying whatever funds he may have borrowed

112 *Real Estate for Active Investment*

to buy it, and leave the investor with a satisfactory annual profit after meeting these expenses. This profit can take on various forms. Not all of the financial benefits of owning an income property come in the guise of cold cash. Moreover, a successful realty investment also implies the ability to sell a property at a profit at some desired point.

Though they differ in many respects, residential and commercial properties have many similarities. To begin, both must be purchased with utmost care. They both not only must occupy land (except in the rare instances of air rights), but they must bear a definite economic relationship to it. They must contain usable space which has a definable value in the marketplace, even though this space is marketed in different units and through different channels. Both require the constant attention of the owner, even if he chooses to retain a managing agent for the property. And, both must be financed with mortgages.

Selecting a piece of residential real estate for investment is a process that must necessarily start with a thorough knowledge of an area. In earlier sections, we suggested that acquaintance with the neighborhood flows naturally from the fact that the investor also lives in the area. This was sufficient when we considered real estate for use as well as investment. But now, we have gained sufficient sophistication to regard a prospective property investment as a venture apart from our daily lives. Therefore, it would be unwise to limit ourselves to our familiar environment. And while there are serious impediments to buying and operating a property hundreds of miles away from home, it is also unwise to restrict ourselves to a narrow geographic range on the other extreme. Decisions will be made quite naturally from the line of inquiry through which we hope to arrive at a number of investment candidates.

REAL ESTATE BROKERS

One very obvious source of prospective purchases is a reliable real estate broker, and one should begin with him. Brokers who have been in business for a number of years can generally be considered reliable. An added measure of safety would be to check his identification as a Realtor, a title that can be used only by members of the National Association of Realtors. Realtors are members of the Real Estate Board in their local community, and the Board, in turn, is a member organization of the NAR and, in most states, of the State Association of Realtors.

The simplest way to begin your search, then, is to visit a broker and explain to him that you wish to invest a given amount in a piece of income-producing real estate. Undoubtedly, he will first inquire into your investment objectives. Are you looking for extra income with a minimum of risk? For a tax shelter? For capital appreciation? For an inflation hedge? Or, it could even be for a combination of these reasons. You must be clear in your own mind. Perhaps the most risk-free way to derive income from your savings is to deposit them in a savings institution. But, as we all know, interest income from savings plans does not protect us against inflation. Also, interest income is taxable. And, your capital will appreciate only slightly through the compounding of interest. Still, fine distinctions have to be made. You must provide your broker with enough information to lead him—and you—to the right avenue of approach. If your regular source and size of income is such that additional dollars each year will make life more enjoyable or will help you meet some of your financial commitments, then you should be clear on that point. If, on the other hand, you have no foreseeable need for added cash return, it may well be that you are looking primarily for capital appreciation and a hedge against inflation. Should you be fortunate enough to have so much direct income that you must find ways of reducing the income tax bite, then a **tax shelter** is what you are looking for. Candor in this regard is important, for much of what you tell the broker will help him and you determine both the type of property to be acquired and the best method of acquisition.

Most likely, the broker will also ask you about any preference you may have between residential and commercial real estate, or if you are interested in a building venture. So let us look at each in terms of the investment objective, recognizing that there is no such thing as an investment without some inherent risks. It is an elementary fact of economic life that return *is* commensurate with risk.

RESIDENTIAL OR COMMERCIAL PROPERTY

A novice in real estate can be expected to feel more comfortable with a residential property, such as an apartment building. The reasons are obvious. Without much business experience, we know that every family must have a place to live. For many reasons, there are both families and various groups of unmarried individuals for whom it makes sense to rent living quarters rather than to own a house. We know, therefore, that there is a market for rental apartments in virtually every urban community. The specter of vacancy does not loom very large. This is not to say that all apartment buildings are thriving enterprises, but, with his back to the wall, almost any intelligent adult could feel capable of finding tenants for his apartments. It is a readily understood type of property. Admittedly, lease commitments in apartments are relatively short. Terms of three years or less are the rule. Some tenants even move out after less than a year, with or without suitable compensation for the landlord. Yet there is an innate comprehension of the marketplace and therefore an innate faith that apartment tenants can be readily replaced.

Pitted against this sense of safety are the more complex requirements of operating an apartment building successfully. It is, for one thing, a continuous merchandising task. The building must always be kept attractive, since there is almost always one apartment that may become vacant and must be rerented. There are numerous basic services the landlord must provide, both under local law and within the competitive climate of the

114 *Real Estate for Active Investment*

rental market. Then there are the chores of bookkeeping. Rents must be collected and applied against the recurring and nonrecurring costs of operating the building. Maintenance is as complex as the building itself, and, it should be recognized, apartment buildings *are* fraught with complexities.

Tenancies in office, retail, and industrial buildings run for longer leasing periods. Although they also must be kept attractive for economic viability, they pose fewer maintenance problems in that tenants are partly responsible for some of the upkeep. Industrial and retail buildings, in particular, rely largely upon the occupants for much of the day-to-day housekeeping. Office buildings are somewhat more akin to apartment houses in this respect.

Yet for all their simplicity, commercial properties present new problem areas for the novice investor. Leases may run for longer terms, but they are also far more intricate. Furthermore, the inexperienced owner may be hard put to know where to find tenants and how to negotiate with them.

Apartment buildings lend themselves to most investment objectives, but they are usually sought for their income potential. Depending upon the community and the neighborhoods within each community, apartment buildings are available in many forms. Some are high-rise structures—six stories tall or more—and others are low-rise, or better known as garden apartments, usually no higher than three floors. There are reasons for selecting a low-rise building. Once a building exceeds two stories, the need for elevators becomes evident. Three-story garden units without elevators exist, but are not quite as desirable. Four-story buildings without elevators are outright undesirable, except at low rents, and are too costly to build with elevators because the elevators are underutilized in relation to their cost. Therefore, few four-story residential structures are being built nowadays. Indeed, once we exceed the two- or three-story limit, depending upon local law, construction codes become more demanding. A two-story garden apartment building, notably one with an entrance for each pair of dwelling units, is built under design parameters similar to those of private houses. In terms of construction cost, therefore, garden apartments are far less expensive. But they do occupy considerably more land per dwelling unit because they are spread out over a much larger area than a tall building of comparable interior size. Somewhere between these two types is the "downtown" apartment building, occupying relatively little ground, and built, probably some decades ago, to a height of four or five stories.

THE INVESTMENT

Before choosing the type of apartment building to buy, it is best to scan the offerings in light of the investment itself and then to determine whether the particular location, building design, and the property's overall condition meet your requirements. A good starting point is the amount to be invested. Let us assume it is $50,000. These funds need not be provided by the

Operating an Income Property **115**

investor alone. He might consider a partnership with a friend or relative. As we have seen earlier, leverage plays an important part here. Considering that a sound property can carry a first mortgage of 60 percent of the value and that a second mortgage can provide as much as another 20 percent, the $50,000 available cash may represent only 20 percent of the total price. Tell this to a knowledgeable broker, and he will start scanning his listings for a property available for sale at approximately $250,000. What can you get for this amount? Much again depends upon the age of the building, the location, and the rent scale that results from the combination of these two factors. To arrive at a benchmark, one should work backwards. This process is known as *capitalizing a return.* (We are assuming now that the investor is interested primarily in income.) When we capitalize a return, we start with the yield from an investment and decide what this investment is actually worth. Then, to be doubly sure, we prove this against another form of capitalization to make certain that we are playing in the right ballpark.

If we have a right to expect that, under current market conditions, a residential property should yield a 12 percent return before depreciation, then our $50,000 investment should bring a return of $6,000. It is also reasonable to expect that a property of this type, free and clear of all mortgages, should yield 10 percent. A $250,000 building, therefore, can be expected to have a free-and-clear net profit of $25,000 a year. Thus we have capitalized in two ways, and we now know that the difference between the $6,000 and the $25,000 must carry the cost of mortgage financing. That difference is $19,000 a year. If, for the sake of discussion, we are to strike an average of 9.5 percent interest for the first and second mortgages, we can capitalize that $19,000 to represent $200,000 in mortgages. This plus the $50,000 investment should buy the $250,000 property. This is not to say that it works out that simply, but it gives us a quick calculation of what we can buy with $50,000.

CASH FLOW

In rough form, then, let us consider what the cash flow of such a building will be and see if it will produce enough to support the anticipated return. **Cash flow,** as we defined it earlier, is the sum of all the income or "outgo" a property produces, including cash and non-cash income or "outgo." This includes money for amortization of the mortgages as well as depreciation of the structure. At the end it should provide a yield of 12 percent to the investor. But this is not enough. It must also provide us with amortization money for the mortgages. Let us assume that the first mortgage calls for 9½ percent interest and 2½ percent amortization for a constant payment of 12 percent. A first mortgage of 60 percent of the total property value is $150,000. Interest and amortization of 2½ percent, therefore, comes to $18,000. And while the second mortgage need not be amortized, it may have to be paid off after five years. Let us say that the second mortgage

116 *Real Estate for Active Investment*

represents 20 percent of total value, or $50,000. To set aside enough funds for its retirement in five years, the building must also produce $10,000 a year for this purpose. Interest on the second mortgage of 13 percent is $6,500 a year. And there are taxes. Based upon earlier examples, let us assume that they come to $12,500. Finally, we should reserve annually 10 percent of the rent roll for maintenance and vacancies. As we shall see, this amounts to $7,400. Here, then, is the cash flow the building must produce:

12% constant payment on $150,000 1st mortgage	$18,000
13% interest on $50,000 2nd mortgage	6,500
Reserve to retire 2nd mortgage in five years	10,000
Taxes	12,500
Heat and utilities	10,000
10% allowance of rent roll for maintenance, repairs, and vacancies	7,400
Depreciation of $200,000 structure over fifty years	4,000
12% net return to investor on $50,000 investment	6,000
Projected cash flow	$74,400

Where is this cash flow going to come from? Rents. Let us assume that in a middle-class neighborhood, apartment rentals average $60 per room per month, or $720 a year. On this basis, the building must contain approximately 103 rooms. These will probably be grouped into units ranging in size from 2 to 4¼ rooms. Let us use an average of 3½ rooms for each apartment. This means that this building contains about twenty-nine apartments with each tenant paying an average rent of $210 a month, which is, in fact, somewhat low. In other words, this could be a building in a relatively modest neighborhood. Or, if the rents were somewhat higher, such as $75 per room per month, they could offset the higher operating costs that they would require. If rents are higher, the building has greater value, and this will be reflected both in higher real estate taxes and a larger reserve for maintenance. The building may, in fact, be worth more than $250,000. The figures shown above are, at best, very conservative.

For the moment, we will not pursue the economics for the second five years, when the second mortgage is retired. These calculations were made simply to prove that the investor with $50,000 available is on the right track when he searches for a $250,000 apartment building containing about one hundred rooms with monthly rentals no lower than $60 a room.

It stands to reason, therefore, that when a broker offers you a building with this general profile, he is making a sound proposition.

EXAMINING THE PROPERTY

There are many variations, and they should not throw you off course. A building in an exclusive residential area might contain only one-half the number of rooms (fifty), but the neighborhood might command rents of

Operating an Income Property **117**

$120 per room per month. But if it were the reverse, or two hundred rooms at $30 a month, you should be careful, you might be looking at an incipient slum.

Now we are getting into the selection process. How the cash flow of $74,400 is arrived at may not seem important, so long as it is there, but this is not really true. For instance, fifty rooms cost less to heat than one hundred rooms, but the tenant paying $120 a room will not settle for the same paint job as the fellow paying half the price. He is going to demand satin finish on all trim and millwork, such as moldings, windowsills, and doors. The tenant paying $60 will let you get away with a single coat of matte paint on everything. In the more exclusive building you may find carpeted halls and more expensive refrigerators and stoves. In the larger, lower-rent property you may need more manpower, such as a handyman or a porter to assist your superintendent. It is also likely that the building with the higher rents is considerably newer and needs less general maintenance. Rent levels often reflect the age of the building as much as they reflect the overall neighborhood. If the building is aging, it may require major replacements, such as a new furnace, and many smaller replacements, such as refrigerators, which may mount up to a major cost item. Enough of these can throw the original calculation of 10 percent for maintenance, repairs, and vacancies into a cocked hat.

THE "SET-UP"

It is necessary to examine a building physically with great care. The question is: At what stage do you make the physical inspection? The recommended procedure is to examine the broker's offering in terms of the "set-up" he presents at the outset. The broker's set-up is usually a one-page presentation which briefly describes the property, including the plot, the structure, its age and location. The description of the structure should provide information about the number and size of apartments, indicating the distribution of rooms among the units. A photograph of the property is usually attached. The twenty-nine-unit building might contain eighteen apartments with 3½ rooms, five apartments with 3 rooms, five with 4 and one with 5. There are untold numbers of variations. Next, the set-up will describe the existing mortgage or mortgages, showing the current outstanding principal, the interest and the amortization terms on each. Property taxes are also stated. This is followed by a summary of rentals, which lead to a "bottom line," or the projected income to the owner. Set-ups always work out on paper. Even if provided by a reliable broker, they sometimes fail to show some of the shortcomings of the property since, after all, the information has been provided by the prospective seller. The only realistic use of a set-up is a quick examination to see whether the offered property evokes any interest in the prospective buyer. If it does, the investor should arrange to personally inspect the property; this is the only way he can know for sure if the property is as desirable as it appears on paper.

118 *Real Estate for Active Investment*

THE PHYSICAL INSPECTION

If he has little or no previous experience, he should take along a friend with some insight into residential real estate. This first visit should merely confirm the impressions gained from the set-up. To make your visit meaningful, you should walk through the building, floor by floor, including the cellar. If possible, you should examine a typical apartment; open a random window to see if it works. You might be wise to spend half an hour near the front entrance to get a look at some of the tenants—and even at the automobiles they drive—as they enter or leave. Inconclusive as they may be, these samplings do provide an insight into the type of building and neighborhood. Then take a walk through the vicinity itself, noting, in particular, the stores. The merchandise they display and the price tags for such things as apparel give clues that can sometimes be valuable. If the owner, the superintendent, or some other representative of the landlord is in evidence, tell him frankly who you are and why you are there. But under no circumstances should you discuss price or any other aspects of a transaction with any of them at this stage. However, do ask questions. Turnover can be a critical factor, so try subtly to verify some of the data in the set-up, such as the expiration of the leases and the length of time most tenants tend to stay. Ask about heating fuel consumption. But do not, under any circumstances, indicate how strong your interest in the property really is.

THE APPRAISAL

If this walk-around leaves you more interested than before, it is time to retain two experts. One is a real estate appraiser (be certain he is independent). Most appraisers are also brokers, but do not hire the broker who offered you the property in the first place. An independent appraiser's function is to make a report which, after all facts about the property are ascertained and stated, arrives at a fair market value—the price you should pay. Not all appraisers think alike, and it is said among realty professionals that three appraisers will arrive at three different valuations for the same property, though they should be reasonably close in price. Indeed, in the purchase of an extremely large property, more than one appraiser is used, and an average of their findings is considered.

There are two schools of thought about the choice of an appraiser if the property involved happens to be far from your home community. One theory holds that the appraiser should come from the general area in which the building is situated, since he is familiar with area trends and has more insight into the future of the particular neighborhood. Another is based upon the concept that an outsider, sent to the area from your community, takes a fresher look at the surroundings and obtains his most valuable soundings by checking more carefully into recent realty sales near the building in question. Actually, both are acceptable choices, and it is largely a matter of the investor's faith in his appraiser and the source that recom-

Operating an Income Property **119**

mended him. In either case, an appraiser will make a physical examination of the structure and all its mechanical equipment, obtain data about the leases and rents paid, and finally investigate recent sales of comparable properties in the area. By capitalizing some of the rental data and applying the results against this information, he will provide you with his report. The appraisal will usually state three values, one for the land, one for the structure, and the combined market value of the property as a whole. But remember, you didn't hire a detective. To a large degree he will rely on information supplied to him. Nor is he an engineer. But he may describe the boiler, for instance, in terms of its brand and age, and may even venture an opinion as to its general condition, as he will about all of the building's appurtenances. For the $2,500 you should expect to pay for an appraisal of a twenty-nine-family building, you will receive an important essential —the price you can feel secure in paying if you decide to buy.

If that appraised market value comfirms or even exceeds the $250,000 price being asked, you should go further. If it falls below, you must make a choice. You may consider buying the property if it can be bought for no more than the appraised value, and hopefully for even a little less. Or you may decide that something is amiss and drop it. Remember, too, that the seller has had either an appraisal of his own before setting a price on his property, or he has sufficient real estate experience to know what the property should be worth. In either event, if you decide to pursue the building further, you can test the seller by making counter-offers below his original asking price of $250,000. If he knows, by appraisal or otherwise, what the fair market value is, you will find that he will gradually retreat to it. At $210,000, for instance, the building may be a good buy. If the seller retreats even below the price of your appraisal, be careful. He may be in financial distress and ready to sell at any price that will solve his problems of the moment. But be careful. His financial distress may have been caused by this particular property, in which case you would want no part of it.

GETTING LEGAL ADVICE

Before you enter upon the bargaining process, you are well advised to consult your lawyer. It is a well-known tenet of the legal profession that a lawyer should be involved in a property purchase from its inception. Lawyers claim, quite correctly, that it is difficult to extricate a client from mistakes he made flying solo at the outset of a realty transaction. Moreover, a lawyer is an excellent intermediary, or shock absorber, in the bargaining process. He can speed it up or slow it down, depending upon the progress of your own deliberations. Even while the appraisal is being made, or just after you have looked at the building physically, your lawyer can check into the status of the mortgages. The names of the lending institutions are sometimes given in the broker's set-up. If they are not, your lawyer can make the necessary inquiries without exposing you as the interested party. What you will want to know, primarily, is the payment record of the

120 *Real Estate for Active Investment*

mortgagor, the present owner of the building. If he has been delinquent in his payments, you can rest assured that something is wrong. Perhaps it is difficult to collect rents in the building and, as a result, the money is not always available when mortgage payments are due. Or there may have been costly repairs to drain off the mortgage money. When it comes to testing the seller's willingness to go down in his asking price, a lawyer can do the best job, because he never needs to commit himself, by saying that he must consult with his client, who can remain unnamed. Even if you are known to the seller, you will be insulated against hasty decisions in this way.

INSPECTION BY EXPERTS

Let us assume, however, that the appraisal has confirmed a market value of $250,000. The first asking price may well have been higher than that. Now the time has come for a close physical examination by an expert. This might be an engineer or a building contractor in whom you or your lawyer have confidence. Better yet, you might turn to specialized building inspection services which have appeared in various parts of the country in recent years. These services, charging a fee of about $500 for a building of this size, are staffed by engineers who do virtually nothing but make inspections for buyers or mortgage lenders. Following their detailed examination, they render a long report of every structural and mechanical component of the building. The report will clearly indicate what repairs are immediately necessary, or should be expected in the foreseeable future. It will cover everything from cellar to roof. While these inspectors are reluctant to give you an estimate of the cost of recommended repairs, it should be easy for you or your lawyer to obtain such cost estimates from a contractor. Once again, if the inspector's report contains negative evaluations which cast a pall on the building, you have two choices: one is to abandon the purchase; the other is to use the projected repairs as a bargaining point when negotiating a purchase price. Let us assume, however, that the building passes the engineer's muster and that your final offer of $250,000 has been accepted via your attorney.

THE MORTGAGE

While all this has been going on, you and your lawyer will have consulted about the existing mortgage or mortgages on the property. In the cash flow computation shown earlier, we have supposed that you would obtain new mortgages in the stated amounts and on specific terms. In actual practice, this may not be necessary or advisable. For example, the property may presently have a first mortgage on it of, say, $120,000. Its face value, when originally made, may have been more, but $120,000 is now the outstanding principal. If that mortgage was made some years ago, it may have a lower interest rate on it, reflecting the interest rates prevalent at that time. It may be to your advantage to take this loan over because of its favorable interest

Operating an Income Property **121**

rate. It may well have eight more years to run, which, from your standpoint, is nearly as advantageous as the ten-year term of a new mortgage and certainly more desirable in terms of the interest rate. Your ability to take over the existing first mortgage depends, of course, upon whether it is assignable under the terms of the bond. Let us say that it is assignable, and look at the implications.

ASSUMING THE MORTGAGES

With a first mortgage of $120,000 and your ability to invest $50,000 in cash, a second mortgage of $80,000 is necessary to complete the deal. In our earlier computation, we assumed that a lender will give you a second mortgage equivalent to 20 percent of the property value, or $50,000. This leaves us $30,000 short. But don't despair, there are four options open to you:

1. You can shop for a second mortgage of $80,000. This may not be easy, since it represents 32 percent of the total value, and would be a substantial risk for someone whose security, or collateral, has a senior claim upon it. We shall discuss second mortgages later, but suffice it to say now that the first mortgage is the senior lien against a property. If you do, indeed, find a lender willing to provide a second mortgage of $80,000, you will find the interest rate to be quite high, possibly as much as 15 percent. As we learned before, the rate of return is commensurate with the degree of risk. So perhaps we can do better.

2. To bridge the gap of $30,000, the seller might agree to give you a so-called **purchase-money mortgage.** In effect, he would lend you the money to make the deal on terms you can afford. In this instance, his would be a third mortgage, standing behind the first and second mortgages in rank of seniority, so his risk would be still greater than that of the holder of the second mortgage. Does this mean that his rate of interest would be even higher? Not necessarily. If he is anxious enough to sell the building, it may be worth his while to keep the interest rate reasonable. It is, incidentally, good proof that he thinks highly of his property, since he will now have to depend upon it to get his money back with interest.

3. In the same vein, you might explore the possibility of obtaining a purchase-money mortgage of $80,000 from the seller. This would be quite a concession from a typical owner of this type of building. From his point of view, the risk is high, and since it serves only to make the deal possible, the interest rate you can afford to pay will not compensate him for the risk. In such a case, he might make a counter-suggestion. It might be to make it a mortgage of $90,000, thus raising the price to $260,000. Actually, you will

122 *Real Estate for Active Investment*

still pay $50,000 cash, subject to the first mortgage of $120,000, but you will pay interest on a $90,000 second mortgage rather than one of $80,000. As we will discover in a later section, he can then sell his second mortgage at a discount for, say, $80,000, enabling the purchaser of the loan to reap a higher effective interest rate. To you this means paying interest on a larger loan and reserving enough out of cash flow to repay the larger amount when it comes due.

4. Finally, you may want to consider what is known as a **wrap-around mortgage**. As the term implies, the second mortgage is wrapped around the first. It means that the seller remains responsible for the payments on the first mortgage. You, in turn, pay him enough interest and amortization to cover his costs on the first mortgage of $120,000, plus a satisfactory interest rate on the remaining $80,000. This gives the seller the option of selling the entire mortgage package to another investor, a subject for a later discussion. Here, too, the total value of the wrap-around mortgage may be higher. The first mortgage has a current value of $120,000; the implied second mortgage is $80,000, making a total of $200,000. The seller may agree to a wrap-around of $210,000 to make the package salable.

One thing becomes obvious. If you follow any of these routes, your combined annual charges for interest and amortization must remain consistent with the cash flow of $74,400 and still yield your hoped-for return of 12 percent, or $6,000 a year. Let us look at this a little more closely. Of the total cash flow of $74,400, some $34,500 was earmarked for *mortgage service*, another term for the cost of interest and amortization of mortgages. Any combination of first, second, third, or wrap-around mortgages that can be serviced with $34,500 a year should lead to a satisfactory deal.

Perhaps, too, your main objective in buying the building is for something other than annual income. This means that you might settle for less than $6,000 a year. The difference would then be available for additional mortgage service, enabling you to be more flexible. What are those possibilities? Let us first consider appreciation. If the building is reasonably new, and if the neighborhood is stable and possibly still on the ascendancy, the property may be worth more than $250,000 when you choose to sell it some years later. Assuming no decline in neighborhood values, a resale should at least reflect the inroads of inflation at a rate of about 10 percent. This means that after five years you should be able to sell it for about $375,000, or for $500,000 after ten years. This is a sound hedge against inflation. If the property is sound and well located, inflation will also enable you to raise rents. A higher rent roll commands a higher resale price, bearing in mind that your maintenance costs will also rise due to inflation. But if this is a particularly desirable neighborhood, you may be able to reap an even larger capital gain through the sale of the building. It is important to remember, in

Operating an Income Property **123**

this context, that the tax on a capital gain is less than that on ordinary income earned as the property's annual yield. However, this is where tax shelter comes into play.

TAX SHELTERS

If you are making your investment primarily for its ability to shelter your other income from income tax, let us see what this building can do for you. Based upon the valuations we have used, it is safe to assume that the appraiser will find the land value to be about $50,000. The structure, the only thing that can depreciate, should be worth $200,000. Taking straight-line depreciation, the same amount each year, over a useful life of fifty years, this means a tax allowance of $4,000 a year. This means that only $2,000 of the $6,000 yield is taxable income. Then, too, there are more advantageous forms of depreciation, such as declining-balance, double-declining, and sum-of-the-digits. These are complex calculations, but in essence they enable you to take the bulk of your depreciation in the early years and less each year as you go along. These depreciation methods have merit, primarily if you intend to sell the property when the depreciation, and therefore the tax shelter, drops to an unsatisfactory level.

Bear in mind, however, that tax shelter is tax postponement, not tax avoidance. Ultimately, if you ever sell the property, you must pay a capital gains tax on the amount of depreciation you have taken. For instance, you have depreciated your $200,000 building at the rate of $4,000 for ten years and now intend to sell it. The book value of the building is now down to $160,000. The land, worth $50,000 at the outset, does not depreciate. You paid $250,000 for the whole property. If you sell it after ten years for $300,000, its total book value will be down to $210,000. While your cash profit may be only $50,000 (bought for $250,000 and sold for $300,000), the capital gain in the eyes of the tax authorities will be $90,000, the difference between book value and sales price. On that $90,000 capital gain, your tax will range from 25 percent, or $22,500, upward, according to your overall income tax bracket.

Having considered all these possibilities, you may find it to your advantage to negotiate for a new first mortgage on the property, as well as for a second mortgage. Based upon the original structure of the deal, the second mortgage would be one of $50,000. In this instance, you may get a better rate of interest from the seller by way of a purchase-money mortgage, than you would by taking out a second mortgage from a professional financing concern.

THE SALES CONTRACT

Let us say, then, that with the aid of your lawyer you have obtained the necessary mortgage commitments, and you are ready to shake hands on the deal with the seller. You can shake hands over the telephone or by mail. In fact, your lawyer may just shake hands with the seller's attorney. It doesn't

124 *Real Estate for Active Investment*

matter. What matters is the contract that must now be drawn. The following does not purport to be a quick lesson in law. But these are the elements which should be set forth in the sales contract:

1. The property and all that is to be conveyed with it should be clearly defined. The type of deed you will receive at the title closing should also be specified. There are many types of deeds, but the most common is a **bargain-and-sale deed.**

2. The consideration, or price you pay, must be spelled out. It must be described *exactly* as to the method and time of payments to be made. It is usual to pay 10 percent of the purchase price on contract. This would be $25,000.

3. The contract should spell out the mortgages, subject to which the property is being bought, notably if the seller is providing a purchase-money mortgage. This clause is important in that it affects the refundability of the down payment.

4. As for refundability of the down payment, this must be stipulated also. If, for example, the seller cannot deliver clear title to the property, the purchaser is entitled to receive his down payment back. If, on the other hand, the buyer fails to go through with the purchase, he may have to forfeit the money which is, after all, a good-faith deposit. It is here that particular care is needed. The reasons for the buyer's failure to complete the transaction determine the refundability of the down payment. For instance, the contract should specify that, even if the seller considers the title to be clear, the buyer must be equally satisfied that good title is being conveyed. Moreover, if the contract makes the sale contingent upon the buyer's ability to obtain the mortgages as described, his inability to get satisfactory mortgage loans may be an acceptable excuse for not buying the building, and thus he is assured the return of his money.

5. The time and place for the title closing should also be set in the contract, but there should be provision for reasonable postponements by either side. The purchaser may need some extra time in the event that either his title search is not completed on schedule or if there is some delay in obtaining the mortgages. The normal time lapse between contract and title closing usually is one to three months.

These are by no means all of the elements of a real estate purchase contract, but the details are best left in the hands of a lawyer. Once the contract has been signed, you should begin to make your financing arrangements. With the help of your lawyer, you should nail down the commitments you have from mortgage lenders. They will, of course, need to see the contract, and may also ask for documentation of the property's financial statements.

Operating an Income Property **125**

These statements, showing rent income and all the expenses, are part of the materials you have already gathered in your investigation of the property before you decided to buy it. While you're busy obtaining your mortgages, your lawyer will undoubtedly be instituting a title search. Without going into the intricacies of title examination, let us take a brief look at what is involved.

THE TITLE SEARCH

In the office of the County Clerk, or a similar local official, there is a permanent record tracing the ownership history of the property. It will reveal its ownership from the days when the Indians dwelled upon the land, show every owner thereafter who has had title to it, and what has been built upon it. The title search will show every mortgage or other lien ever placed against the property, and how each of these claims was eventually satisfied. At the end, it should show the seller to be the true and sole owner of the property, with no encumbrances other than the mortgage or mortgages to which he said the property is presently subject. Any other liens or breaks in the chain of title would open the title up for question. For example, a previous owner may have left the property to his three children. If, subsequently, the property was sold by only two of them, there must be adequate explanation of what happened to the third, lest he or his heirs appear on the scene some fine day to claim an interest in the building you thought you rightfully owned. The search will also show whether the property is subject to any easements granted, such as (ridiculous as it may sound), the right given to a railroad to run its tracks through the middle of the building. The railroad may have ceased to operate eighty years ago, but if the easement is still in force, it may constitute a defect in title. If the record lacks a satisfaction for an earlier mortgage, its repayment must be established or the lien may still be valid. There may also have been restrictive covenants at one time. If one should show up, indicating, for example, that the property may not be used in any way except as a house of worship, it is important to check the record for the revocation of that convenant. If never revoked, the apartment house should not be there, but this is not your problem unless or until you buy it.

It may seem like a title search is a cumbersome and gargantuan process. In a sense, it is. But it is normally handled by so-called title companies, whose searchers are adept at these things. Moreover, when clear title is certified, you would normally purchase a title insurance policy. Under this type of insurance, for a one-time premium payment, the title company insures you against any loss in the event a defect in title should be discovered later and someone asserts a claim against the property. The amount of the premium depends upon the total value of the property, as well as the complexity of the search. Sometimes some money can be saved if the search and insurance are in the hands of the same title company that insured the seller. In this event, the search can begin at the point at which

126 *Real Estate for Active Investment*

the last examination left off. In other words, it would only seek to find any encumbrances or other flaws incurred since the last policy was issued to the present owner. In some cities and counties, the **Torrens system** is in use. This is a system whereby the title search is automatically kept current even if a property is not conveyed, thus enabling you and the title company to obtain an immediate reading of the title's quality.

TITLE CLOSING

With the mortgage financing in hand and title search completed, you are ready for the title closing. This is a meeting at which the deed to the property is transferred from the seller to the buyer, and it is normally attended by both parties, their lawyers, representatives of each of the mortgage lenders involved on both sides, and an agent of the title insurance company. Perhaps the most important thing to remember is the principle that all agreements, in the contract or otherwise, merge in the title. Once you have accepted the deed, you have no further recourse to anyone, except if a fraud has been perpetrated. Therefore, everything must be in order when the parties sit down around the table to close the title. That table, incidentally, might be in the office of one of the lawyers, at one of the banks involved with one of the mortgages, or at the title company. The arrangements are usually made by the lawyers.

Assuming you are buying the property under the terms of the original example, let us look at who brings what to the closing:

1. You, the purchaser, arrive with a copy of the contract and a certified check for $25,000, which is the remainder of your cash investment, since you paid $25,000 on contract. That check is made out to the seller, be it an individual, a partnership, a nominee, or a corporation or trust. You also bring your checkbook with a balance sufficient for other payments that will be described a little later.

2. The seller arrives with his deed to the property and a certified check for $120,000, payable to the holder of his present first mortgage.

3. The holder of the seller's first mortgage arrives with the original of the mortgage and a letter of satisfaction of that mortgage.

4. The lenders who are giving you the first and second mortgages come to the table with their mortgage instruments ready for signing. For each mortgage there are two basic instruments: a bond and a mortgage, which may be combined into a single document. The bond is basically your I.O.U. in the amount of the loan. The mortgage is the document which asserts the lien, or claim, against the property, identifying the property as the collateral for the loan. In your case, there will be two mortgage lenders,

Operating an Income Property **127**

each armed with the papers that constitute bonds and mortgages for $150,000 and for $50,000, respectively. The first mortgage is identified as such, claiming seniority over the second mortgage in case of a default leading to foreclosure.

5. The seller's lawyer joins the group with a survey of the property. This is an official map, derived from the county's tax map, showing exactly what the boundaries are.

6. Your lawyer should have prepared what is known as a *punch list*, a list of items which should be cleared up before you accept title. Some of these are legal points. Others may be questions you have raised during your final personal inspection of the property, such as the whereabouts of a vital piece of equipment or the seller's failure to repair something as was promised. Remember that all promises merge in the title.

At the outset, all parties around the table examine each document to satisfy themselves that everything is in proper order. What then follows is more legend than fact. In theory, all papers, properly signed and notarized, waft gently through the air and simultaneously land in the hands of the various parties. In actual practice, the papers are passed around the table for needed signatures and do not reach the intended holders at the same time. But the effect is much the same, since everybody remains at the table until the entire transaction is concluded. When it is, the following will have occurred:

1. The first mortgage lender will have given you a check for $150,000 and you will have signed the bond and mortgage for that amount and given them back to him.

2. The second mortgage lender will have done the same, giving you a check for $50,000 and receiving your signed bond and mortgage.

3. You will have given those two checks plus your certified check of $25,000 to the seller, who now has three checks worth $225,000. This, with your earlier down payment of $25,000, will equal his selling price of $250,000.

4. The seller will have handed the deed to you.

5. The seller will also have made out a check for $120,000 to discharge his first mortgage, and will have received an instrument of satisfaction from his mortgage lender.

6. The agent of the title company will have handed you a title insurance policy and you will have made out a check for the search and premium.

7. You and the seller each make out checks to your respective lawyers for their trouble.

8. The representatives of the three mortgage lenders and the title

128 *Real Estate for Active Investment*

company agent will then rush out of the room to the County Clerk's office to record the effects of the closing. The holder of the seller's mortgage will record the satisfaction, thus removing the liens from the property. The two parties who gave you the new first and second mortgages will record the new liens against the property. The title agent will record the new holder of the title —you.

ESCROW

Before all this can occur, however, a few details must be attended to. As we said earlier, there is the punch list. If, for example, the seller had agreed either verbally or in the contract that he would repair a plumbing leak and then failed to do so, this must be settled before all agreements disappear in the title conveyance. This type of thing requires brief negotiation. The simple solution is to establish an **escrow** account for such items. In effect, you hold back an agreed-upon amount that will cover the cost of the item in question. In actual practice, your check for $25,000 is already certified, so it cannot be altered at the table. It is easier, therefore, for the seller to deposit a separate check for that amount with one of the lawyers, to be held in escrow against this outlay. The seller could also agree to lower the final price of the property by that amount, but this would cause untold rewriting of the various documents, and this is seldom done. It would almost certainly entail an adjournment of the title closing to another day.

In any event, escrow checks are not the only ones to be passed across the table. There are a number of adjustments to be made. For example, the seller may have prepaid some of his utility bills or fire insurance, but you, as the buyer, are responsible for electric bills from the day of closing. So you owe him something. There may also be some oil in the tank which you, as the new owner, will now use. You owe him money for that. There may be some outstanding bills from painters, plumbers, and gardeners for work done for the seller. These bills are now your responsibility, but they are the seller's debt. So he owes you the money for these. Therefore, before the final title conveyance takes place, these adjustments must be made by the seller, the buyer and their lawyers. A balance is struck between what you owe the seller and what the seller owes you. The escrows for unfulfilled obligations are included here. At the end, the result will be a check passed in one direction or the other.

When you finally do walk out of the room, you are the owner of a $250,000 apartment house.

MANAGING YOUR APARTMENT BUILDING

An entire volume could be written about the management of apartment buildings, and experience has shown that hired professional management may well be worth its price either if the property is very large or the owner

Operating an Income Property **129**

is totally inexperienced. We will attempt here only to provide some guidelines for the investor.

At the outset, let us assume that the building was properly managed by or for the previous owner. If he is a real estate professional who devoted all of his time to the management of this and other properties, he probably managed it alone. If not, he probably retained the services of a professional manager. Most likely this manager is a partner or employee of a real estate firm who allocates some of his time to property management along with sales and rentals as a broker. If he has done a satisfactory job for the previous owner of the building, he may well provide the same service for you. Lacking such an individual, you may wish to turn to the broker who brought you and the seller together and consider him, or someone he recommends for the assignment.

In the financial set-up of the property, we did not consider the cost of management. But the cash flow was predicated on rentals of $60 per room per month which, in today's market, is conservatively low. In the same building, an average rent of $70 per room per month would bring the cash flow up to $86,520, a difference of $12,360, which should be ample for management. Let us see why. A professional manager will attend to the property for about 2 percent of the rent roll, or about $1,700 in this instance. That leaves about $10,600 for the services of a superintendent, either on a part-time or full-time basis. Not all of this need be paid in cash, since the superintendent normally occupies rent-free quarters somewhere in the building. Normally, it is one of the smaller, less desirable apartments in the building. A superintendent needed for a property of this size is primarily a mechanical aide, and by no means a resident manager in the full sense of the term. While he will collect the rent, he should not be expected to maintain the accounts or be held responsible for the financial management of the building. If it is the investor's intention to have a full-fledged resident manager on the premises, he will have to consider paying him upwards of $12,000 a year, including a rent-free apartment. In this event, he will also need a handyman or porter for such chores as taking rubbish to the street, cleaning the halls, and the like. However, with only twenty-nine apartments, a resident manager might also be shared with a neighboring building.

It should be quite apparent that no two situations are exactly alike, and that much depends on how the previous owner handled the matter. To help make this decision, let us briefly review the landlord's various responsibilities and outline the options he has for coping with them.

1. RENT COLLECTIONS Basically, this is a simple matter of preparing twenty-nine rent notices, each showing the rent due for the month. These can be slipped under each tenant's door or into his mailbox. In some buildings, this is not even done. Tenants in many buildings are accustomed to bringing their checks to the superintendent's apartment, or mailing them to the owner, man-

130 *Real Estate for Active Investment*

agement agent, or superintendent, according to the instructions given at the outset. Only when a tenant is delinquent is it necessary to remind him to pay his rent, either by telephone or a visit to the apartment. In many cases, a superintendent can collect the rent. Depending upon the owner's wishes, the superintendent will deposit the rent—checks, money orders, or cash—in a conveniently located bank and maintain a simple record. (A professional manager, of course, will keep more detailed records.) It is enough to provide him with a list of tenants, showing the amount of rent due monthly from each tenant. When he receives the rent, the superintendent checks it off, keeping the bank deposit slips to verify his collections. If at all possible, the owner should avoid handling his own collections. It exposes him each month to all kinds of tenants' requests for special services and considerations which he may not wish to grant. It is always best to have a buffer between the tenants and the landlord, thus making it easier and less personal to deny such requests.

2. LEASING When an apartment is about to become vacant or a lease is due to expire, an early effort should be made to find a new tenant. Depending upon the terms of the existing lease, the tenant is normally obligated to notify the landlord, managing agent, or superintendent of his intentions to renew his lease. If the lease does not provide specifically how far in advance the apartment may be shown to prospective new tenants, the superintendent or manager should make arrangements with the present tenant to show the apartment. At the same time, you should consider how much rent should be charged for the apartment. A managing agent knows what the traffic will bear, provided there are no rent control laws in effect. Lacking an agent, you can sometimes rely upon your superintendent's knowledge of the neighborhood, where rents are established through recent rentals in similar buildings. It is debatable whether a landlord should quote the hard-and-fast rental of an apartment or ask for somewhat more, with the intention of going down if need be.

Once a new tenant has been found, a lease should be drawn. Perhaps the simplest way to prepare a lease is to purchase a standard residential lease form in a commercial stationery store. However, your lawyer should go over it with you and make such amendments as he deems necessary before you offer it to a tenant. We must assume that, in the purchase and operation of a $250,000 property, you will continue your relationship with your lawyer for a variety of reasons. If, on the other hand, you retain a managing agent, he is also quite capable of preparing a suitable lease when it becomes necessary. He is also best qualified to negotiate the rental with the prospective tenant. Although the superintendent may be able to get the lease signed, its terms should not normally be left in his hands.

Operating an Income Property **131**

When a tenant decides to renew his lease for another term, the task is much simpler. The only major decision that needs to be made is the price of the rental, a determination which can be made by either the landlord or his managing agent. Sometimes a continuing tenant may request some special services at the time he renews his lease. He is probably entitled to a fresh paint job anyway, but he may ask for special colors or wallpaper or some other minor improvement. If such requests are not exorbitant, you may wish to grant them, considering that you have saved the cost of finding a new tenant or of even carrying a vacant apartment until a new tenant has been found. Experience is a good teacher in such instances; a professional managing agent is an even better one.

3. LEGAL AND ACCOUNTING As the owner of a building that houses twenty-nine families, you are never without need for some legal and accounting services. There are a number of municipal authorities with which the owner of an income-producing property, and notably a multiple dwelling, must deal regularly. There are housing and building laws by which you must abide and violations you must avoid. And, considering the number of people who enter and leave the property daily—not to mention those who sleep there nightly—various insurances are necessary to protect you against lawsuits. (Even then, you can never be immune from legal actions.) This means fire insurance, liability coverage against accidents, and many other types of necessary coverage. You will have no problem finding willing insurance agents to provide you with the coverage you need. And if you have a professional manager who is in the real estate business, chances are that he also handles insurance. For a better assessment of what he offers you, consult your lawyer. He is familiar with both the risks and the potential consequences.

Accounting, too, becomes a complicated matter without professional help. It is not only the question of maintaining accurate records of rent collections and expenses for everything from light bulbs to boiler repairs, but it is also a matter of paying the proper taxes and local assessment fees and of making decisions which may affect those taxes. Remember that a property of this sort requires much more attention to detail than a one- or two-family house in which the owner usually pays a single monthly sum to the bank that provided the mortgage. The bank, in turn, parcels out the various real estate taxes—city, county, school taxes—as they come due. With an income-producing property, the owner or his agent pays each of these authorities separately. If it appears that the property carries too high a tax assessment, your lawyer or managing agent will know where to turn with an appeal for a reduction. Then there are payroll deductions, Social Security taxes, and Workmen's Compensation which must be withheld

132 *Real Estate for Active Investment*

from salaries and deposited in special accounts. Even if you plan to handle these items yourself—assuming that you have the services of a secretary or assistant as part of your basic business —you will need direction from your lawyer or accountant.

There are also some subtle decisions that may affect the income tax you eventually pay on the return from your investment. One of the first and most basic is the decision of *ownership format*. For example, you may wish to own the building in your name as an individual. In terms of taxes, this has an advantage, in that you avoid payment of a corporate income tax which is levied against the corporation's income before you take any of it home. On the other hand, personal ownership imposes the risk of personal liability in the event any catastrophe results in claims larger than insurance will cover. The same is true of a partnership if you are buying the property with somebody else.

However, if you incorporate the property, you are protected in that only the assets of the corporation—the land and building —can fall prey to such claims. In a partnership, limited partners also enjoy this immunity, but somebody has to be a general partner, with full exposure, and this will be your role if you are the primary investor. The principal drawback of a corporation is its obligation to pay taxes on its income before any of it is distributed to the one or more shareholders as dividends. This means that the net yield is reduced substantially, depending upon the applicable tax rate.

In some cases, a real estate trust is the answer. As we will learn later in a discussion of realty trusts, they are somewhat similar to corporations. They afford certificate holders—in effect, stockholders—the same protection against personal loss. Moreover, the income from a real estate trust is immune from corporate taxation if at least 90 percent of the cash flow is distributed to the shareholders. In any case, it is obvious that the advice of both lawyer and accountant is important from the outset.

There are other decisions of this kind which must be made from time to time. The question of whether any given outlay for repairs or improvements is to be "expensed" or "capitalized" is one of these. To some degree, the decision is not entirely yours, your lawyer's or your accountant's. The government provides rulings on such situations. But to the extent that you have a choice, what are the relative advantages?

Expensing an outlay of this sort means that the total cost of the item is applied against the profit-and-loss statement for the year in which it occurs. This tends to reduce the taxable income in that year. When the item is capitalized, the total cost of, say, a new furnace is written off over a number of years, usually the length of time for which the furnace will be useful, despite the fact that you

Operating an Income Property **133**

have paid for it in full at the time of installation. If a major item is expensed, it reduces the taxable income from the property in that year, but offers no tax shelter in future years. On the other hand, in future years the profit-and-loss statement will not again be burdened by the cost of the furnace.

If you plan to resell the building in the next few years, it is better to keep the expense item off the books and to show the maximum return on investment to the next prospective owner by capitalizing the outlay. If, however, you plan to own the building for a long time, a little bit of tax shelter through capitalizing may also save you tax money. This is clearly a decision best discussed with your lawyer and accountant. Depreciation is a matter of the same ilk. Since there are several methods of depreciation that can be established for the building, the tax consequences of each method should be carefully weighed, as you will have to remain consistent once you have set a pattern for such accounting principles as depreciation and expensing.

4. MAINTENANCE AND REPAIRS The paramount consideration is, again, consistency. Whatever you do for one tenant, you must be prepared to do for all the others. It is impossible to provide an investor with a total maintenance manual in a few pages. Nor is it feasible to predict the need for repairs for each property. Obviously, the public areas—entrance lobby, halls, stairways, elevator, laundry rooms (just to name a few) must be kept clean, well lit and in nicely decorated condition. Under most local laws, and certainly as a matter of good business, apartments should be painted on an average of once every three years, usually coinciding with the signing of a new or renewed lease. Mechanical equipment must be kept in good repair. This includes not only the major installations, such as the heating plant, roof, plumbing, and electric lines, but also landlord-owned appliances in the apartments themselves. The amount of repair the superintendent or handyman should provide the individual tenant becomes a matter of discretion. The building's owner is responsible for changing washers in bathroom faucets and easing a jammed window sash, but not for changing light bulbs for his tenants. And, as the owner, you can rest assured that the superintendent or handyman will perform some of these chores on your time if the tenant offers him a gratuity, and you had better resign yourself to the fact that there is little you can do about it.

There is a seemingly endless list of maintenance tasks to which the superintendent must attend, and we will not go into them here. But what we must consider are the guidelines for when tradesmen should be called in. A good superintendent can change a washer, but when it comes to unclogging a particularly obstreperous drainpipe—especially if it means ripping up a tiled

134 *Real Estate for Active Investment*

bathroom floor—there may be a problem. Although a plumber will charge for it, he may save you money by limiting the peripheral damage to the floor in the process of getting at the affected pipe. Electricians should be called in for many services which the handyman can easily handle, because the invoice from a licensed electrician can be critical if a fire is subsequently attributed to an electrical repair. His certification by Underwriters' Laboratories as a professional may make the difference in absolving you from blame if a lawsuit arises from the fire. If you have a professional managing agent, you can usually be certain that these decisions will be made in your best interest, though you should always be consulted if there is any doubt.

Consultation with you, the owner, becomes even more important if a major repair such as replacement of the roof or boiler, rewiring or a major plumbing job looms ahead. Your advisor—in this case the managing agent or possibly even the superintendent—should lay all the options before you. He should suggest various ways of doing the job—a complete rehabilitation or a limited repair—and show you estimates he has already obtained from qualified contractors. Your lawyer should also be consulted to make certain that if compliance with the law is involved, you are not risking violations by taking the less costly way out. Even your accountant might have an opinion on the financial and tax impact of a major repair, and whether it should be expensed or capitalized. But the ultimate decision must be yours. And, armed with the facts, you will be able to make the best decisions and, as time goes on, become more self-reliant in these matters.

The problems of maintenance vary little between different types of buildings. While a high-rise building may require more sophisticated equipment such as an elevator and a large boiler, it is also more compact. When we speak of a twenty-nine-family building, it would certainly be no more than six stories tall. It is beyond that height that a building requires a significant degree of engineering know-how. A garden-type development of two or three stories is constructed similarly to two- or four-family private houses. Essentially a chain of attached houses, they usually contain a series of small heating units. Some units are even heated by individual heaters in each apartment, especially in the warmer climates. Still, their maintenance and service are the landlord's responsibility. At the same time, a garden-type development requires more attention to landscaping, since the buildings are surrounded by lawns and play areas. In many cases, garden apartments provide for enclosed parking. Garage space is a separate source of rent revenue which can be a financial advantage, since garages require virtually no maintenance. Generally speaking, garden apartments require less sophisticated mainte-

Operating an Income Property **135**

nance than do taller buildings. By the same token, they may call for a little more low-skill manpower because they are spread out over a larger area.

Until now we have based this discussion upon the financial results of the first five years of ownership. We established that, with a rent rate of $60 per room per month, there is a budget of $74,400, including 13 percent interest of $6,500 on a second mortgage of $50,000 and an annual reserve of $10,000 to retire that mortgage at the end of five years. This left a yield of $6,000 on an investment of $50,000, or 12 percent. At the end of the fifth year, the second mortgage is retired, thus ending the annual payments of $16,500 occasioned by the existence of a second mortgage. However, this money will now be needed for repayment of at least part of the first mortgage of $150,000 when it comes due at the end of ten years. Let us see how this works.

TEN YEARS LATER—MORTGAGE DUE

The face value of the first mortgage was $150,000. If the constant-payment rate of 12 percent included 2½ percent amortization, the outstanding principal will have been reduced at the rate of $3,750 a year or a total of $37,500 after ten years. At this point, therefore, the outstanding principal, or balloon, will be $112,500. If during the second five years the now available $16,500, formerly used to pay off the second mortgage, is now reserved for repayment of the first, $82,500 will be on hand to reduce the balloon. When the tenth year expires, therefore, the original first mortgage can be replaced with a new mortgage of only $30,000. It should be easy to obtain, and will cost only $3,600 a year. During the second decade, then, the budget will look something like this:

12% constant payment on $30,000 first mortgage	$ 3,600
Taxes	12,500
Heat and utilities	10,000
10% allowance for vacancies, maintenance, and repairs	7,400
Total expenses	$33,500
Rental income	74,000
Return to owner	40,500

This is a yield of 81 percent. However, as in any of the examples we have used, we have assumed that none of the basic conditions have changed during the ten years of ownership. We must consider many possibilities. Mortgage interest rates may vary, and possibly increase. Taxes are almost certain to rise. Repairs and maintenance may become more expensive, too, especially as the building ages. At the same time, rents should also rise, reflecting at least the impact of inflation and hopefully other favorable neighborhood factors. Even if the neighborhood has lost some of its appeal, the owner can still reap a handsome return on the strength of average rents of $40 to $50 per room per month.

Chapter 12
Operating an Office Building

SELECTING A BUILDING

Let us now translate this example into an investment in an office building of similar value, approximately $250,000. Basically, we can assume that with a cash investment of $50,000, a first mortgage of $150,000, and a second mortgage of $50,000, such a building can be purchased. In this instance, it becomes necessary to check the validity of the price by a different method. Office space is not rented on a per-room basis, but rather by the square foot. To attain a cash flow of about $74,000, we must first see how much space such a building must contain.

If we consider $7 per square foot per year a low-to-medium rental, it would take about 10,500 square feet to accomplish our purpose. To build a new office building with 10,500 square feet should cost approximately $20 a square foot, or $210,000. This leaves $40,000 for land value. This may appear to be a low estimate, but modern office buildings, notably those on the fringes of the city, are usually two-to-three stories tall, and consequently not too complex in terms of their construction. Taller—and usually older—office buildings in downtown areas have a higher *replacement cost*, which is the cost of building an exact duplicate from scratch. But when you buy an older structure of this type, you must make an allowance for age, and not think in terms of replacing it with an identical structure.

Operating an Office Building **137**

In some ways, of course, office buildings are much simpler structures than apartment buildings. They do not have kitchens and baths for every tenant. Interior partitioning is normally an initial investment only, since tenants must pay for changes they want in their office layouts. In a broad sense, therefore, we can establish the fact that $250,000 will buy an office building with about 10,500 square feet of gross rental area, and that such a property will yield upwards of $74,000 in annual rents.

CONSULTING A REALTOR

Once again, the services of a Realtor are almost essential in finding a suitable property of this sort. But the criteria of location are certainly different from those of a residential building. It must first be determined whether there is an existing commercial life in the area or whether the neighborhood, if newly developed, has the potential of attracting new tenants. If the building is downtown, a broker can aid you in sizing up the rentals in comparable offices on surrounding blocks. This decision must include an assessment of whether the area is largely inhabited by a particular industry, such as insurance, banking, and the like. Buildings near the courthouse, for instance, will attract law firms. Other spots may be a focal point for importers, or branch offices of insurance companies. On the edge of town, newer office buildings attract branches of local utility companies or new firms requiring rapid access to the local airport. There is no single yardstick for the selection of an office building for investment.

LEASE TERMS

One of the benchmarks that plays a much larger role is that of lease terms. Unlike apartments, office space is rented for periods of five years or more, except in the most marginal of buildings—the type you would certainly want to avoid. There are many reasons for this. An office tenant—a substantial firm of the type you would want in the building in the first place —makes an investment of its own when it moves in. As we pointed out before, the tenant pays for the partitioning and, to some degree, special fixturing. This is especially true if he requires equipment such as computers, whose installation is by no means cheap. He invests in such seemingly minor things as return-addressed stationery and business forms which, when added up, come to a pretty penny. Finally, his new office address represents a certain value in good will, both toward his customers and his employees, as well. Although the business community tends to hold the peripatetic enterprise in low regard, the office tenant also usually provides some escape routes in his leasing arrangements. In almost every such lease, a sublet clause is provided for. This enables the tenant to move if business conditions mandate it. If, for example, he outgrows the space he occupies and there is no way of expanding within the building, he must either move or split his operation between two locations, which is usually an undesirable solution.

138 *Real Estate for Active Investment*

The sublet clause, however, is coupled to the clauses which clearly define his rental obligations to the landlord. These obligations center on the tenant's duty to pay the rent for the full lease term. Regardless of what happens to his sublessee, he is liable for the rent during the interim. And if the sublessee, for any reason, fails to pay, the landlord can look to the original tenant to pay the rent. Thus, it should be quite obvious that the credit investigation of an office tenant must be far more intensive than it would be for an apartment tenant. After all, it is also more difficult to evict an office tenant, not so much in the legal sense as it is physically. Office equipment cannot just be collected and thrown out onto the sidewalk. And if the tenant goes into bankruptcy, his space may have to be kept intact while the authorities come in and liquidate the business. In such an event, you, as the landlord, become a creditor and, most likely, a victim of the circumstances.

Although there are lease forms to be purchased for use in renting an office, you are best advised to retain your lawyer to draw the proper lease as the owner of an office building. The cost of his services can be far less than the consequences of a mistake in judgment or lack of experience.

MAINTENANCE

The problems of maintenance in an office building also vary from those in an apartment house. There is a definite need for some sort of professional management, but not in the form of a resident superintendent. Most offices are used during the daytime only, and the lease should include any special charges that may be incurred as a result of nighttime use. There are, of course, no recalcitrant stoves or showers to fix, but there are washrooms and other appurtenances. If there is an elevator, its maintenance is usually performed regularly under contract by a professional elevator maintenance company. If heating and air conditioning are a central installation, they must be supervised by a qualified engineer. Depending upon the size of the building, this engineer may be a full-time employee, or he may be shared with a neighboring property. One thing, however, redounds to your benefit as an owner. In an office building, if your superintendent or building manager is called upon to make repairs inside a tenant's premises, those services—including the replacement of light bulbs and other supplies—are charged to the tenant at the end of each month. This is true even of cleaning services. Whether you hire a cleaning crew of your own or retain a professional cleaning service, you, as the landlord, are responsible for only the public areas (the halls, washrooms, elevators, and accesses to the building). If a tenant uses either your cleaning services or those of an outside contractor, he is billed for it.

FINANCING

Keeping in mind these differences between office and residential buildings, let us look for a moment at the financing problems for an office building. As indicated before, it is entirely possible to obtain a first mortgage of $150,000 on an office building worth $250,000 in the marketplace. In the eyes of the mortgage lender, however, an office building and an apartment building are two different animals. The security of an apartment house, as far as a lender is concerned, is the innate need for apartments at reasonable rentals in a neighborhood that tends to attract families with incomes to pay these rents. The mortgage lender does not worry excessively about vacancies, knowing that there will always be a family for each apartment so long as the building is properly maintained. Not so in an office building. Changes in business trends, neighborhoods, and prevailing rental rates can make a seemingly safe building risky as an investment—for both the mortgage lender and the investing landlord. Therefore, both must have faith in the property. (Heed these words; they apply to you, as the investor, as much as they do to the mortgage lender.)

Before committing himself to a mortgage loan, a lender will want to know about the quality of each office tenant, including his financial stability, the length of his lease, and particularly about his remaining term and renewal options. If, for example, he is considering your application for a ten-year mortgage, he will scan your leases to see if they will cover your payments for interest and amortization over the next ten years. If all of the leases were to expire before ten years with no renewal options, he will be loath to grant the loan. An ideal building, therefore, is one in which a major tenant occupying a large amount of the space is obligated under a long-term lease of ten years or more. If that tenant is financially sound, and can be relied upon to pay the rent even if he wants to move out and sublet, he represents an important asset in the eyes of a mortgage lender.

Staggered lease terms are also important. It is a bad omen if all or most of the leases expire at about the same time, forcing the landlord to search for a whole new complement of office tenants. And what about the prospects of renewal? These vary according to the type of business occupying the space. A service business—an employment agency or small public relations firm—can easily move, because their only equipment is desks and file cabinets. Other types of tenants with major equipment installations have the aforementioned investment in the premises and, given reasonable renewal terms, are usually inclined to stay rather than face the costs and dislocations of a move.

If you are assuming the mortgage already existing on the building when you buy it, the lender's original deliberations may not always be available as a guide to you as a buyer. But if you are negotiating for a new mortgage, he will do some of the important thinking for you. If he considers the roster of tenants—or their lease arrangements—too risky for a $150,000 first mortgage, you may assume that they are also too risky for you to acquire the responsibilities of a $250,000 property.

In an earlier chapter, we discussed office buildings for use as well as investment. Let us return to that thought for a moment. If you are in business and intend to occupy a major portion of the building for your own operation, you may well become the major security for the mortgage

140 *Real Estate for Active Investment*

lender. This engenders an entirely different line of thinking. But if, under the premise of this chapter, you are investing in an office building for investment's sake only, a tenant roster which does not satisfy a mortgage lender should not satisfy you, either. This does not mean that you should succumb to the first lender's opinion. Make a second application elsewhere. And if the dice come up the same way again, you are well advised to walk away from the deal. This is why it is important to shop the mortgage market even before you deposit good-faith money on a contract with the seller.

Usually, however, a prospective mortgage lender will not turn you down cold. He may make a counter-proposal of a $100,000 mortgage, feeling that the building will be reasonably good collateral to at least that extent. This would mean a cash down payment of $150,000 unless you can obtain a second mortgage or purchase-money mortgage for $100,000. If the prospective seller makes such an offer, do not be lulled into what seems like a friendly accommodation. He may be so anxious to get rid of the property that he may go a long way to help you out. He knows the property's failings. He knows that, if he does nothing, he will lose in due time whatever equity he may have in it. By lending you $100,000 in the form of a purchase-money mortgage, he still stands to lose some or all of it, but in the meantime, he has received your $50,000 cash investment and may see himself coming out better than if he did nothing. To be certain, ask the prospective lender of the first mortgage if he would risk the $100,000 on the basis of a purchase-money mortgage from the seller of an equal amount. A good guess is that he will decline it and possibly caution you against accepting.

CHOOSING THE OCCUPANTS

From all this, one would have to draw the conclusion that office properties are not as quixotic as apartment buildings as investments. Their tenants, if properly selected, are usually more stable than apartment occupants. But when they depart, they are also more difficult to replace. It might be said that operation of an apartment house can be a pack of little troubles and an office building presents fewer problems but usually bigger ones. This is not to say that both are not good investments. It is merely a way of helping the investor find the optimum property for investment in either category. In the case of the apartment house, good references for each new tenant help assure a large degree of stability. In an office building, an exhaustive credit check provides a major safeguard. Another safety device is the avoidance of a one-industry building. Beware of filling up an office building with tenants in one industry. If that industry suffers reversals beyond your control, bankruptcies and vacancies could ensue.

Negotiating leases with office tenants is somewhat more complex than it is for apartments. In an apartment house, the landlord may set a certain rental for a given apartment when it becomes vacant (provided there are no rent controls in effect in that municipality). That rental should not only be

Operating an Office Building **141**

in consonance with prevailing rates in the neighborhood, but also should not be unfairly high or low in relation to rents paid by other tenants, because word *does* get around. But if a particularly attractive tenant views the apartment and tries to shave a few dollars off the rate, the landlord's decision is easy to make. If he is anxious to rent the apartment, he can make a small concession just to end the vacancy, as long as he does not go so low as to infuriate other tenants in similar apartments. In an office building, this procedure becomes somewhat more complex, since space is leased by the square foot and since improvements, such as partitioning, are negotiable.

As we discovered earlier, office rentals are based on either the gross or net rent per square footage. The net represents only the space actually used by the tenant. The gross takes into account his share of the public areas, including the halls, downstairs lobby, elevator shaft, and the washrooms. Gross rent per square foot is lower than net rent. But, applied to a given piece of office space, they come out to approximately the same amount. This provides an ideal negotiating point. How much public area do you wish to load into the lease you are about to negotiate? If a particularly appealing prospect looks at the space and balks at the gross rental rate, you can compromise by lowering the amount of gross square footage—the amount of public space—you will allocate to his occupancy. Or you can offer him a net space lease at a mutually agreeable figure, so long as the final amount is sufficient to meet your requirements in terms of operating the building.

And, there is still another leveling factor. In renting an apartment, a compromise is expressed in lowering the rent by $10 or more per month. In office space, we are dealing in price *per square foot per year*. If, for example, a tenant is interested in a 5,000-square-foot part of a floor, a concession of 20¢ per square foot is a substantial compromise. At the end of the year it saves the tenant $1,000 and gives him a sense of victory. On the other hand, in the financial statement of the property, it merely means that the space was rented for $6.32 a square foot instead of $6.52. This hardly damages the repute of the building to the extent that future lease negotiations must center on a lower figure. When the next prospective tenant comes to look at vacant space, say 1,500 square feet, you can quite properly start by asking for $6.82 a square foot. You will probably never be asked to justify it. But if you are asked, you can simply stand your ground by citing the fact that the $6.32 tenant took a much larger space and earned a small discount on volume.

If you choose not to compromise on price per square foot, you can also offer to share in the cost of the leasehold improvements. Thus, you can offer to supply the doors or some other fixtures in the partitioning, or you can make a special deal in the area of cleaning services, lighting for late evening work, or any of the variables that office buildings, unlike apartment houses, provide.

In sum, an office building is a more complex investment, but it is also a

142 *Real Estate for Active Investment*

more flexible one. In view of this, the importance of relying on real estate brokers and your lawyer cannot be overstated. Nor can one overstate the rewards of good investments in commercial properties of this sort.

MULTI-USE INDUSTRIAL BUILDINGS

These do not differ much from office properties. The major characteristics of such structures are their high-load floor construction to sustain heavy machinery, and the many safety devices which must be built into them. However, the current trend is to single-tenant production space, such as the examples that were cited in the discussion of leasebacks. For this reason, it is best to drop multi-use industrial buildings from serious consideration. True. industrial tenants are even less likely to move than office tenants, because of the cost of transporting machinery and re-installing it elsewhere. But finding new tenants for industrial space in a multi-tenant building is considerably more difficult for the same reasons. Moreover, multi-use industrial structures, also known as manufacturing lofts, are usually found in marginal and often dilapidated sections of most communities, and therefore present problems which the novice investor had best avoid.

Perhaps the best way to conclude a discussion of investment in the active operation of real estate—be it vacant land, residential, commercial, or industrial buildings—is to point out that these investments require considerably more direct attention than do properties bought for use as well as investment. More than any other type of real estate investment, they pave the way for an owner's eventual total involvement in the real estate profession. Those who own two-family houses or rent out their summer cottages can do so with promise that they will reap a monetary reward from their foresight through the years. But those who become sufficiently immersed in realty operations by owning and operating income-producing properties will acquire daily increased insight into the principles and workings of the real estate industry. If, at some point in life, they prefer to leave their primary occupations to devote all of their time and more of their capital to realty, they will be well prepared to embark upon a new career of almost limitless dimensions. In fact, many a lucrative realty career has been carved out of an earlier side venture of this nature.

PART IV
REAL ESTATE SECURITIES

INTRODUCTION

A real estate investment need not involve direct contact with a property. At the very beginning of this book we recognized that money deposited in a savings bank or savings and loan association is, indirectly, an investment in real property. Savings institutions use these deposits to provide mortgage loans for private houses, apartment buildings, and commercial properties. The interest they earn from these loans is then used to pay interest to the depositors. Consequently, money kept in a savings account finds its way into real estate.

Insurance companies do much the same thing. A portion of the premiums they collect is set aside as a reserve against claims, and the remainder is invested, mostly in mortgages, with some of it even going into direct ownership of property. Therefore, anyone who carries insurance also has a stake in realty. What is lacking in both instances, of course, is the individual's choice of the real estate in which the institution makes its investment. Nor has the savings bank depositor or insurance policy holder any responsibility for the way a property is purchased or operated. He is a totally passive investor.

Our purpose here is to examine some of the ways in which a moderate investor can take advantage of this passive role and still reap some of the benefits the world of real property has to offer. Like most investment vehicles, this passive, indirect way of participating in realty is a two-edged sword. On the advantageous side is its relatively small requirement for expertise. In virtually all cases, a professional is involved, selecting the property, the mode of the investment, the amount of funds to be committed, and the way in which the property is to be run. But there are pitfalls as well.

As an investor once removed from the property itself, you have little or no control over its viability. You must rely upon the discretion of others which, though they may be professionals, is, at best, still human judgment prone to human error. At its worst, it can be the judgment of ambitious men who bite off more than they can chew—with the investor's money. What finally emerges here is an investment form in which understanding of real estate must be complemented by a sensitivity to personal character traits and, even more important, a subtler, more sophisticated insight into the intricacies of finance. Land and brick and mortar are no longer the only essential commodities involved. Money and the way it stirs in the yeast of the economy becomes a more important entity than it was in the situations we examined up to this point. Let us see what this means in another context.

SELECTING THE RIGHT INVESTMENT

If one has an abiding faith in the future of the automobile industry, the thing to do is to invest in one of the large car manufacturers such as General

Motors. Clearly no one of us can go out and start building cars. But what kind of investment should one make? What most readily comes to mind is the purchase of General Motors common stock. This has a great deal of merit. There is a modest return in the form of dividends. If the automobile market is strong and the company's earnings rise, the resale value of these shares increases and, in the vernacular, the stock goes up. It is also a hedge against inflation. It has growth potential.

Suppose, however, an investor is more enamored of a steady, guaranteed return on his money than he is in the growth of his equity or an inflation hedge. His best bet then is to buy General Motors bonds. While these can increase in resale value only slightly, they do provide a stable income in the form of interest.

And what if one wants to play a wait-and-see game before deciding which type of investment is best? In this case, there is commercial paper issued by General Motors Acceptance Company which, though short-term, offers an even higher rate of interest. It is still an investment in automobiles, for the GMAC commercial paper finances the consumer's purchase of a car from a General Motors dealer. In each instance, money behaves differently within the confines of the same industry.

So it is with real estate. There are various ways of putting money to work in real estate with different results and for different purposes. There are both growth opportunities and sources of steady income. There are long-term commitments and short-lived interests. And none of these require close association with a property, though there are times when it is best for the investor to have at least a passing acquaintance with the real estate involved. Since we have concerned ourselves so far with realty investment vehicles which do require close attention to the property itself, let us depart from this only slightly at first and examine one type of investment which is only a small step removed from actual ownership. This is the **second mortgage.**

Chapter 13
Second Mortgages

In previous chapters we have already seen how second mortgages are required to help bridge the gap between the price of a property and that part of it which can be financed with a first mortgage. We have seen it in the examples of the retail store building, the property with professional offices, the industrial property, and the larger office building. We have also come to recognize that, for the purchasers of such real estate, the **second mortgage** creates leverage with which a relatively small amount of money can buy a large property. Now we are going to jump the fence and see how that second mortgage looks from the viewpoint of the lender.

Let us construct a simple example. Somebody wishes to purchase a building priced at $100,000. He is able to obtain a first mortgage of $60,000, which represents 60 percent of the total price. On the face of it, he would seem to need $40,000 available, or he may prefer the leverage of buying the property with only $20,000. This means he needs an additional loan, known generally as a second mortgage. There are essentially two ways in which he can obtain a second mortgage. One source is a professional lender of second mortgages. The other is the seller of the property. If the seller is sufficiently interested in disposing of the property, or if the immediate cash is not of primary importance, he may provide the mortgage himself. In this case, it is known as a **purchase-money mortgage** but, to all intents and purposes, it is a second mortgage.

Second Mortgages **147**

It is time now to look carefully at what a mortgage is, rather than what it can do in enabling someone to buy real estate. A mortgage really consists of two legal instruments—a bond, or note, and a mortgage.

BONDS

This is little more than an I.O.U., an instrument which conveys a sum to a borrower and sets forth the terms by which it is to be repaid with interest. It specifies the length of time the borrower may keep all or part of the money, the rate of interest to be paid, and the amount of principal to be repaid at stated intervals.

MORTGAGES

The mortgage itself is a lien, a legal claim against the property in the event that the conditions of the bond are not met. This makes the property the collateral for the loan. In some cases, depending upon the terms of the mortgage, it may even act as a personal claim against the owner of the property or against a third party who acted as a guarantor. Therefore, when we deal with mortgages, we must always keep in mind two things: the way in which money is lent and the property which acts as security for the loan.

As a practical matter, then, we have dual considerations in looking at a mortgage under the financial microscope. We must first be certain that the purpose for which the funds are lent—in real estate it is property—is one which will enable the borrower to do profitably what he set out to do and still leave him with enough money to repay the loan with interest. Second, we must assure ourselves that the property, the collateral, is always worth at least as much as the amount the borrower owes the lender at any given moment. In the case of an income-producing property, the two considerations are closely interwoven. As long as the property is doing its job for the owner by earning sufficient income, it is likely to be worth at least what the owner owes the lender.

In a private house, this is not quite so true. The borrower, or homeowner, wants only to have a comfortable place for his family to occupy. The value of the property, therefore, is not contingent upon the income it brings in. This is why lending institutions look to the income stability of the home buyer rather than that of the property when they provide mortgages on homes. As for the property's sustained value, they must rely upon the buyer's willingness to maintain it attractively, and on the prognosis that the neighborhood will remain desirable for residential use. But it is a different story for commercial real estate.

COMMERCIAL REAL ESTATE

To understand this concept more fully, let us return to the case of the $100,000 property, and then translate it into the interest of a second-

148 *Real Estate Securities*

mortgage lender. As shown earlier, the buyer of such a building can obtain a first mortgage of $60,000. Let us say it is a ten-year loan at 9½ percent annual interest and calls for 2½ percent of amortization, or repayment, each year. This is a constant payment of 12 percent a year, or $7,200. In addition, the owner obtained a second mortgage of $20,000 for a term of five years. For purposes of this discussion, let us assume that it calls for 13 percent interest a year and no amortization. Why the big difference in interest rates between the first and second mortgages? We will see shortly.

We do know that the lender of the second mortgage must collect $2,600 during each of those five years. In total, this means that the property must throw off $9,800 a year just to meet its obligation on the two mortgages. This $9,800 must be available after the owner has collected his rent, paid the property taxes, heated the building, and attended to all of the required maintenance and repairs. In addition, the $9,800 should be available after all these costs have been met and still leave the owner with a fair return on his own investment of $20,000, of, say, 10 percent, or $2,000.

THE ECONOMICS

Let us look at the "set-up" which would make this possible. On the most conservative basis possible, this is what the set-up might be on a $100,000 commercial building.

The basic facts to be assumed are that the $100,000 property consists of $20,000 in land and an $80,000 structure. If such a building can be produced for $20 a square foot, it should contain 4,000 square feet of rentable space, which in a favorable location should bring $7.50 a square foot a year. This means the following:

Real estate taxes (property is assessed at $50,000 and the tax rate of $10 per $100 of valuation)	$ 5,000
Heat	1,500
Maintenance	6,000
Constant payment on 1st mortgage	7,200
Interest on 2nd mortgage	2,600
Owner's return on his $20,000 investment in property	2,000
Annual reserve for repaying 2nd mortgage of $20,000 in five years	4,000
Available for retirement of 1st mortgage during first five years	1,700
Required cash flow first five years	$30,000

This means that for the first five years, at least, the property must yield at least $30,000 in rents. An average rate of $7.50 for 4,000 square feet would accomplish just that. After that, the lender of the second mortgage is out of the picture and really should not worry any more. But to complete the picture, let us see what happens after the first five years, when the interest and reserve on the second mortgage fall away. We should know this to

Second Mortgages **149**

establish the health of the property even more firmly.

Let us keep in mind that, during the initial five years, the owner was able to set aside $1,700 a year toward repayment of the first mortgage as well. This totals $8,500. Moreover, he is repaying 2½ percent of the $60,000 first mortgage during each of the ten years of its life, or $1,500. By the time it comes due ten years hence, it is already paid down to $45,000, $8,500 of which was reserved during the first five years. During the second five years, then, he must reserve another $36,500 to repay the entire mortgage. In his budget, the figures will look like this:

Taxes	$ 5,000
Heat	1,500
Maintenance	6,000
Constant payment on 1st mortgage	7,200
Owner's return on investment	2,000
Available for retirement of 1st mortgage	7,300
Required cash flow second five years	$29,000

At the end of five years he had $8,500 reserved for repayment of the first mortgage. During each of the second five years he set aside $7,300 for this purpose, totaling $36,500 needed to eliminate the first mortgage altogether, with $1,000 a year in cash to spare if rents bring in $30,000 a year. This raises his return on his $20,000 investment to 15 percent during the second five years. Furthermore, the investor may seek a new first mortgage of, say, $50,000, which should be readily available, and use these funds while he gradually repays the loan over the second ten years.

An investor in a second mortgage—or really any mortgage—must check these figures to ascertain whether such a loan would be a good investment. In the example given here, he now has assurance that there is enough money to pay his interest over the five years and that the owner has ample reserve funds from the property to repay the $20,000 when it comes due at the end of the five years. He is further assured that the owner derives a satisfactory return on his own investment, thus keeping him happy and interested in the welfare of the property. What remains to be seen is whether the building can actually generate the $30,000 cash flow needed to accomplish all this. This requires a knowledge of the rental market where the building is situated. As the lender of a second mortgage, the investor must be assured that space in such a building will bring $7.50 a square foot a year and that there is, in fact, sufficient demand for the space at all.

As an investor in a second mortgage, especially an investor with limited experience, you would be foolhardy to make a loan commitment on a structure yet to be built. You should look only at existing and operating properties where the cash flow has already been established. In most cases, this means buying the mortgage from the original lender, a point which bears more detailed discussion a little later. However, to make an intelligent mortgage decision, one must look at the leases. First, this includes an

150 *Real Estate Securities*

examination of the tenants, their financial stability, and the length of their leases. A branch office of the American Telephone & Telegraph Company under a twenty-year lease is obviously preferable to a five-year lease with a small consulting firm. Most investors would rather see rents of $7.25 a square foot from AT&T than $7.75 paid by a nondescript little business enterprise. And one should remember that sound, long-term tenants often pay less per square foot than less stable businesses with a shorter lease commitment. This is why one must look at the average rent per square foot and the average length of tenancies to get a clear picture. It is an average of $7.50 a square foot which makes this particular building pay off. But it would be far from ideal if literally all of the space were rented to large space users on long terms. This would leave the owner with virtually no flexibility when one of the good tenants decided to expand his offices and pay a premium for the added space, since there would be no space due to become available for a long time. This inability to expand within the building in the foreseeable future may impel such a prime tenant to move elsewhere. True, he would continue to be responsible for the rent for the rest of his lease term, but he may install a far less desirable subtenant in the premises and bring down the quality of the building.

These are subtle determinations, to be sure. But the investor in a second mortgage does not have to go it alone. There is, after all, the judgment of the owner of the property whose interests are parallel. Even more valuable is the opinion of the first mortgage lender, whose stake is subtantially larger, and who, by virtue of his ability to make such large commitments, can be assumed to make an even more incisive appraisal of the situation. This is not to say that a given building must necessarily be a good risk for a second mortgage simply because it satisfies the owner and the lender of the first mortgage. Even if the owner invests all of his money in the equity, he has almost full control of the physical property and can cut many corners to make it pay off for him. The first mortgage lender looks to the collateral to protect his $60,000, and the collateral must have been appraised at $100,000 to warrant a $60,000, or 60 percent mortgage. Consequently, all the lender of the first mortgage need know is that, in a foreclosure, he could sell the building for $60,000. It would take quite a calamity to render the property worth less than that amount. But what about the holder of the second mortgage?

SECOND-MORTGAGE FINANCING

The property serves as collateral for both loans. But, by definition, the first mortgage is the senior lien. If both lenders were to exercise their claims at the same time because of the owner's default in payments, the holder of the first mortgage would have the first right to foreclose. In so doing, he would try to recoup his $60,000 either by selling or operating the building. If he sells it for no more than his own investment, the holder of the junior lien, the second mortgage, is out in the cold. If the foreclosure sale brings more

Second Mortgages **151**

than $60,000, the excess goes to repay as much of the $20,000 as it will cover. Only if the foreclosure sale brings more than $80,000, the total of the two loans, does the excess go to the owner after all legal expenses and other costs of the foreclosure have been paid. Of course, if the first mortgage has been somewhat amortized—after two years it would be down to $57,000—the remaining principal would be all the first mortgage lender can claim in the foreclosure. The remainder would be available first to the holder of the second mortgage, and, if that is totally satisfied, the remainder would go to the hapless owner.

Therefore, in effect, both lenders are looking to the same collateral to back up their loans. The risk of the second mortgage is greater because its claim on the collateral is subordinated to that of the senior loan. This is why the interest rate on a second mortgage must be considerably higher, since there is always a relationship between risk and reward. The exact ratio, of course, depends upon the economy in general and the money market in particular. If a lot of investors have money available for second mortgages, they will compete for the mortgage by lowering their interest rates. If money for this purpose is scarce, interest rates will rise as, indeed, they do for first mortgages and all other types of lending as well.

In the case of the second mortgage, however, there is the unique need to keep abreast of how the first mortgage is faring. The risk of the second mortgage is greatly increased if its holder is unaware that the owner of the building is having trouble meeting his payments on the first mortgage. Conceivably, he could wake up one morning to find that the first mortgage lender is ready to foreclose, and find himself without collateral—and powerless to do much about it. This is why the investor in a second mortgage must stay abreast of the building's operation, almost as if he owned it. He must be aware of vacancies, of unusual operating expenses, and even the sudden departure of a tenant. If the vanished tenant is held responsible for his rent for the duration of the lease, his failure to pay it would, in turn, leave the owner of the property unable to make his mortgage payments. When this happens, the cycle that leads to foreclosure could begin.

FORECLOSURE

An owner in this position has three desperate choices. He can skimp on maintenance and thereby accelerate the decline of his building, possibly to the point where it will actually become worth less than the total of the mortgages. He can default on his second-mortgage interest, thus inviting foreclosure by the second-mortgage holder. Or, he can default on the constant first-mortgage payments, leading to foreclosure from that source, or he could do all three.

However, the holder of a second mortgage does have a remedy if he is aware of the problems early enough. He can temporarily help the owner make his payments on the first mortgage and thereby choose his own time

152 *Real Estate Securities*

to foreclose before the first-mortgage lender has reason to do so. In this event, the holder of the second mortgage will eventually own the property, subject, of course, to the first mortgage which remains intact. Except for a real estate professional, this is not a desirable prospect, but it does help to explain the reason for the high interest rate of second mortgages. It also gives some clue as to why the holder of the first mortgage need not get too upset if the owner is derelict in paying his interest on the junior loan. If the second mortgagee forecloses, the lender of the first mortgage simply has a new owner to look to for payments, and the collateral is still there to be taken in the event of default.

THE WRAP-AROUND MORTGAGE

None of this is intended to portray second mortgages as bad investments, but simply to explain why they yield such a good return. Of late, real estate professionals developed what might be called a fail-safe way of investing in second mortgages known as the **wrap-around mortgage.** As the term implies, the second mortgage is wrapped around the first mortgage and the risk is thereby reduced. Since wrap-around mortgages are too complex an investment medium for the novice, I will explain them briefly.

In a loan of this sort, the investor, in what would normally be considered the second mortgage, takes on the full responsibility for paying both interest and amortization on the first mortgage. In turn, the owner of the property regards the total of the two mortgages as a single loan payable to the holder of the wrap-around. As a first cousin of the second-mortgage investor, the holder of a wrap-around mortgage has reduced his risk considerably, because he has full control of the first lien and therefore need not fear foreclosure from the lender of the senior mortgage. Given this assurance, he can offer a somewhat lower interest rate and still lend profitably. However, it is a sophisticated investment which naturally follows the experience an investor will eventually amass through the years.

Until now, we have looked at second mortgages in terms of their origin. We have seen how a lender, or investor, offers a five-year loan of $20,000 to enable a purchaser to buy a $100,000 property. Chances are, however, that the small investor will have little opportunity to participate in the origination of such a mortgage. He is not likely to be on the scene when such a transaction takes place, and more importantly, probably lacks the experience to make the best possible judgment in committing his money to such a venture. For both reasons, he is far better advised to buy an existing second mortgage from a professional. Let us see why.

PROFESSIONAL MORTGAGE LENDERS

Professional second-mortgage lenders, be they institutions or real estate concerns, have a limited amount of money available for second mortgages. It may become necessary for them, therefore, to replenish their funds by selling some of the second mortgages they hold and clean out their stock, as it were, to generate new cash. As a result, these mortgages become available to investors. Just as frequently, the seller of a property who provides the buyer with a purchase-money second mortgage disposes of the loan by selling it at a discount to an investor. Let us look at this possibility first, since it will come to the attention of a nonprofessional investor more readily.

Assume an owner wishes to sell an income-producing property that originally cost him $75,000. At the time he bought it, he had a $50,000 mortgage on it that required him to invest $25,000 cash. Now the market for this building enables him to sell it for $100,000, after reaping income and tax benefits from it for a number of years. Through a broker, he finds a willing buyer at $100,000. The seller, broker, or buyer then arranges for a new first mortgage of $60,000, or 60 percent of the price. In addition, the seller is prepared to offer the buyer a purchase-money second mortgage of $20,000, enabling the purchaser to make the deal with only $20,000 of his own cash.

THE TITLE CLOSING

The lender of the new first mortgage gives the buyer $60,000. The buyer, in turn, gives the seller the proceeds of that mortgage, or $60,000, plus his own cash in the amount of $20,000. Finally, the seller provides the $20,000 purchase-money mortgage. Thus, the seller holds $80,000 in cash plus the $20,000 purchase-money mortgage. With the $80,000 cash he pays off the remaining principal of his own first mortgage, which may now be down to $45,000. This leaves him with $35,000 in cash, or already more than the $25,000 he put into the building at the outset. If he can now convert the purchase-money second mortgage into cash, he will have made an attractive cash profit. In fact, he can now afford to sell the second mortgage for $17,500. Since the face value of the second mortgage is $20,000, this would be a discount of 12.5 percent, and he would wind up with a total of $52,500, or a $27,500 cash profit over his original investment.

To sell that $20,000 purchase-money second mortgage, he will probably rely upon the broker who first brought him and the buyer together. After all, a good broker will not only put buyer and seller into contact, but is most likely at least partial author of the way in which the deal is structured. He may have advised the seller on the price of the property, helped him arrange a new first mortgage commitment for the eventual purchaser, and to complete the picture, made some sort of commitment for disposing of the resulting purchase-money second mortgage. This commitment may have taken various forms. As a broker, he may have a group of followers among real estate investors, one of whom is likely to buy the mortgage. If he has a large real estate business, he may have been prepared all along to take that mortgage into his own investment inventory, either permanently or until an interested investor comes along.

154 *Real Estate Securities*

INTEREST RATES

When such an investor comes along, what will he be buying? He will receive a second mortgage with a face value of $20,000. The interest rate might be 13 percent. At 13 percent, a $20,000 mortgage yields interest of $2,600 a year. But the investor is buying that loan at a 12.5 percent discount, or for only $17,500. The interest he receives annually, $2,600, is actually 14.8 percent on his invested $17,500. This is an attractive investment, to be sure. In addition, however, he will be receiving the total face value of $20,000 when the second mortgage comes due, probably after five years. This means that the investor will receive five years' interest, or $13,000 plus the face value of $20,000, for a total of $33,000. If he subtracts the $17,500 originally invested, the five-year yield is $15,500. On an investment of $17,500, this is an annual return of 17.7 percent. Whatever risk a second mortgage might entail, this is certainly an adequate reward for it.

For a novice investor to find such a mortgage is not as difficult as it might seem. Brokers who transact at least some sales of commercial real estate usually have such mortgages, either in inventory or about to be created. In the course of handling property transactions for their clients, lawyers are equally aware of such mortgages when they occur. Moreover, both brokers and lawyers can often structure a real estate transaction in a way that will create such a mortgage, thereby also helping both buyer and seller.

An investment of this sort need not be in a purchase-money mortgage, as we discovered earlier. In fact, once the mortgage leaves the seller's hands, it becomes an ordinary second mortgage. Therefore, if the loan is being sold to an investor out of the real estate broker's inventory, it is an ordinary second mortgage. Having established that fact, we can now think in terms of buying such mortgages from other sources, such as professional second-mortgage lenders.

A firm specializing in second mortgages may have bought the $20,000 mortgage we just discussed. It may have paid $17,500 for it and is prepared to make a short-term profit by reselling it for $18,500 to an investor. The face value of that loan is still $20,000 and the interest rate, based upon face value, is 13 percent, or $2,600 a year. If an investor buys that "paper" at a 7.5 percent discount, or for $18,500, what return will he get on his money? The annual interest alone will be slightly in excess of 14 percent. Let us assume that the mortgage is one year old when the investor buys it. He will therefore receive four years' interest, or $10,400 plus the full principal of $20,000 when it comes due four years later, for a total of $30,400. From this, the investor subtracts his investment of $18,500 and finds his four-year yield to be $11,900. This is an annual return of $2,975, or slightly more than 16 percent. Also pretty good. Why would one buy a second mortgage from a firm such as this to earn 16 percent, when, conceivably, one could obtain a purchase-money mortgage at nearly 18 percent from an original seller? Simply because second-mortgage concerns advertise their wares and are

Second Mortgages **155**

more easily accessible to some prospective investors than sellers, brokers, or lawyers at precisely the moment when such a mortgage is being created.

In purchasing a second mortgage for investment, it is as important as ever to make certain that the collateral—the property—is sound. The mere fact that a professional has created the loan is not sufficient assurance. Bear in mind that this same professional, be he the seller, his broker, or any other party to the property's ownership or sale, is also willing to sell the loan. Consequently, his interests are not inimical to those of the investor. A better source of reliance is the lender of the first mortgage. In most cases, his stake is larger than anyone else's. Therefore, if the property is sound enough for him, it is also good collateral for the owner of a second mortgage—with one exception.

The first mortgage, as we learned earlier, is the senior lien. If anything should go awry, and the property owner is delinquent in his payments on the first mortgage, foreclosure could result before the holder of the second mortgage can look to his security. A good practice, therefore, is to make frequent reporting on the property's operation a condition of the second mortgage. This is a contractual requirement which the investor can demand as part of his purchase of that mortgage. He should demand a copy of the property's monthly statement of income and disbursements, and an audited statement at the end of the fiscal year. In this way the investor will have early warning of any defaults *before* they occur. If, indeed, there is a delinquency in first-mortgage payments for interest and amortization, he should contact the holder of the first mortgage immediately and negotiate ways of curing the delinquency. It is here that an investment in a second mortgage can become costly, for the surest way out of the dilemma is to meet the delinquent payments for the owner of the property in order to avoid the threat of foreclosure. However, it should also be borne in mind that the holder of the first mortgage is not inhuman. It is usually an institution which can afford to make some compromises, an institution which also loathes the need for foreclosure and will take steps to avoid it.

The remedy may take the form of a moratorium on payments until the property owner has worked his way out of the predicament that caused or is about to cause his default. It may also take other forms, such as a short-term loan to the property to meet an unforeseen expense. The owner of the property normally will not interfere with such arrangements, and is hardly in a position to do so, for he may lose the property altogether if he is not cooperative.

Once again, none of this should limn second mortgages as undesirable investments. Rather, one should consider them a fair mirror of the principle that risk and reward vary in direct proportion. A 17 percent return on investment, for example, implies a degree of risk. After all, the investor will nearly double his money in five years, and do so in a fairly stable industry.

Chapter 14
Syndication

One form of investment in real estate "paper" is the so-called **syndication of property.** As the name implies, it is a vehicle for the ownership of property by a syndicate of investors, a group of people who pool their funds for this purpose. We can suppose that the earliest form of realty syndication was a pact between two or more friends or relatives to combine their resources to buy a property of one sort or another. Since then, however, syndication has become far more complex and, to be sure, has had its ups and downs in public favor. It has also become subject to scrutiny by various government authorities, as have virtually all forms of group investment in stocks, bonds, or partnership interests.

The basic difference between a simple partnership arrangement among a few friends and a syndication in its current sense is the professionalism which is brought to bear on the latter. Perhaps we would do best by expanding upon a simple example to illustrate this.

Suppose Joe comes across an income-producing property which he would like to own. Even after a first mortgage has been secured, the purchase would involve a cash investment of $100,000, but he can afford to put up only $20,000. He calls Uncle Harry, his friend Larry, and a few more people in his social circle who have expressed interest in a real estate investment. If five of them can muster contributions totaling the needed $100,000, Joe and his friends can buy the building. If the deal goes through,

Syndication **157**

each will be a partner in proportion to his contribution of money to the venture. If each of them came in with $20,000, they would be five equal partners. But if Uncle Harry contributed $35,000 and Larry only $5,000, Uncle Harry's interest in the partnership would be 35 percent, and Larry's would be only a 5 percent.

In its simplest form, this kind of partnership can work well. But there can also be problems. For instance, if each of the partners were to demand a voice in arranging the purchase of the property and in its daily operation, decisions could become difficult to make. In fact, Uncle Harry, with the most money in the deal and possibly the least knowledge of real estate, could be the dominant voice, and become the one-too-many cook in the kitchen who spoils the broth. But there is work to be done. And if Uncle Harry has the largest stake, will he also be the one to devote the most time to the operation of the property? The chances are against it. He will probably want to sit back and enjoy the return on his investment with a minimum of effort. Obviously, this sort of enterprise must be organized from the beginning if it is to be successful, especially if it is to transcend the "Uncle Harry" concept of random investments.

PROFESSIONAL SYNDICATES

In a professionally organized real estate syndicate, one investor must take the lead for a number of reasons. He must find suitable properties for syndication and negotiate their purchase. He must also manage the property or at least supervise its management by a specialist in this field. The professional syndicator handles the money—the receipts and disbursements as well as the distribution of income to the participants. Most importantly, he sets the ground rules by which the partners will make their investments and by which the distributions will be made. One of the most significant ground rules is in the very nature of the partnership.

If a property is purchased either by an individual or by two or three persons, each of them is aware that he may have to supplement his original investment with additional money if an adverse situation arises, such as the sudden breakdown of the boiler. When strangers invest in a venture, they want to be assured that whereas they could conceivably lose their entire investment, they are secure from any further demands for money, and even personally immune from the results of a lawsuit. Under the laws of most states, individuals or partners in a venture have no such immunity. However, most states also recognize the status of the "limited" partner, who, like the stockholder in a corporation, enjoys the same insulation against liability. Consequently, real estate syndicators have long ago turned to so-called limited partnerships, in which the investors are limited partners. Only the syndicator himself, or group of syndicators, are "general" partners whose liability is not limited. One might well ask the question: why, then, are syndications not incorporated to enjoy limited liability? The answer to this lies in real estate corporations or investment trusts, which we will discuss later.

THE SYNDICATOR

In a syndication, however, the syndicator, acting really as a promoter in the legitimate sense, puts the entire package together. He finds a suitable property and negotiates for its purchase; he arranges for the needed mortgage or mortgages and determines how many partnership "units" need to be sold to investors; he makes the projection of how much each unit will yield to the investor; he eventually operates the building or supervises its management; he takes total responsibility. Some professional syndicators are real estate investors in their own right, others are lawyers who make some investments of their own and who represent clients with real estate interests. More recently, syndications have also been sponsored by securities firms as a way of offering their clientele investment opportunities in addition to stocks and bonds.

Naturally, a syndicator does not do this work for love alone. His remuneration comes in two main ways. He may set up a management company, owned by him, which operates the properties of the syndicates he sponsors, a service for which each syndicate pays. Or, he may cut up the pie of investment units in such a manner as to make him a partner without any cash contribution to the deal. In effect, he looks upon his talent in putting the deal together as a contribution which entitles him to be a participant in the venture—and in its profits.

Another way in which he can profit is by purchasing the property at one price and selling it to the syndicate he forms at a somewhat higher price. None of these methods is illegitimate or even questionable. It is important however, that all of this is disclosed candidly to prospective investors. Federal and state authorities see to it that full disclosure is made. In fact, it is illegal to offer partnership interests to more than twenty-five prospective investors without first registering the offering with the Securities and Exchange Commission in much the same way as new issues of stocks and bonds must be registered. In many states, those syndication offerings which are not subject to SEC scrutiny must still be registered with the state's Attorney General or a special agency established for this purpose. These are safeguards, many of them the outgrowth of earlier abuses in the syndication industry. However, it is safe to say that today's investor in a realty syndicate has more protection than his predecessor of the 1950s.

Since syndication usually involves major properties that often cost more than one million dollars, offerings of limited partnerships are not readily found through neighborhood sources. As mentioned earlier, they are sponsored by large real estate investment companies, some securities firms, and other financial service companies. For the small investor to gain access to a syndication means letting his lawyer, his accountant, or his stockbroker know about his interest. Most of the time it is a word-of-mouth contact until one begins to circulate among the investing fraternity. Although this sounds occult, it is not really the case, but rather that syndication is a sophisticated business, conducted by sophisticated people.

Syndication **159**

A prospective syndicate is advertised only occasionally in the financial pages of a major newspaper, and virtually never in the papers of smaller cities. There are, however, real estate trade journals in which roadsigns can be found. The *National Real Estate Investor*, for example, is almost exclusively devoted to realty investments of all types. While there may be no advertised solicitations for investments, it deals regularly with the activities of major investors who, on occasion, form syndicates. A regular reader of such a publication will eventually become familiar with the names of syndicators and should have no trouble contacting them by telephone or mail. Even if someone who appears to be a syndicator is not actively in the business, he probably will not hesitate to suggest other sources.

THE PROSPECTUS

Syndication offerings are presented to investors in various ways. If participations are being offered to a large number of investors, the basic information about the deal is contained in a so-called prospectus, a formal, printed statement that sets forth all of the details of the investment. In many cases, the prospectus will indicate on the cover page that it has been registered with the Securities and Exchange Commission or with the applicable state agency. If the property is being offered to a smaller, more intimate group, the offering statement may be somewhat more informal. Ideally, it should contain all of the pertinent facts required in a registered offering, but an investor cannot be absolutely certain of this. In any event, he is well advised to consult his lawyer and his accountant about the venture just as he would if he were buying a property alone.

In a formal prospectus, the entire transaction should be outlined to include most or all of the following:

1. A full description of the property to be purchased by the syndicate and the price to be paid for it. It will reveal from whom the property is being bought, and notably whether it is already owned by the syndicator who is selling it to the investors at a profit to himself.

2. The mortgage or mortgages either on the property or about to be placed upon it to finance its acquisition should be fully detailed. This description should include not only the interest rate, repayment schedule and balloon at maturity of each mortgage loan, but should also give any information about prepayment penalties, should the syndicate decide to pay off a mortgage ahead of schedule for any reason, such as wanting to find a less expensive mortgage with which to replace it.

3. All leases should be described, with special attention to the quality of the tenants, the length of each lease term, the rent being paid, in the case of retail tenants, percentage clauses,

160 *Real Estate Securities*

escalation clauses to protect the owners against rising labor costs and taxes, and whatever other information may be pertinent.

4. A complete financial set-up of the property as a whole, including taxes, operating costs, and reserves for vacancies and repairs. This set-up is identical to the summary of operations an investor would seek if he were buying a building for his own account.

5. Any information pertaining to lawsuits against the property, its former owners, or any other suits connected with it. This also should include data about any violations of the building code that may have been placed against the property, with evidence that such violations have been removed. In addition, there should be evidence that the property is properly insured against fire, liability, and all other risks.

6. Perhaps the most significant section of a prospectus is the one which deals with the syndicator himself. Not only should his business background be spelled out beyond a glimmer of a doubt, but the prospectus must make his interest in the venture absolutely clear. If he or his associates are to get a piece of the action without contributing funds of their own, the investors must be told in advance. Moreover, it is likely that the syndicator or group of syndicators will receive a management fee for operating the property. This is perfectly proper, but the arrangement must be spelled out in the prospectus. The syndicators' financial responsibility *must* be proven since they will be the conduit for the money which flows from the building to the investors. If they are having other financial problems, one might have reason to suspect they could be tempted to divert some of the property's income to other purposes, such as bailing out a syndicate of theirs which is not doing so well.

7. The nature of the syndicate is next on the prospectus list. Generally speaking, it will probably be some form of limited partnership in which the syndicator or syndicators are general partners with complete liability, and the investors are limited partners with liability limited to their basic individual investment, just as if they owned shares in a corporation. However, there are pitfalls for which one must be on guard. For example, the sponsors may form a corporation which becomes the general partner. There is nothing wrong with this, provided that the corporation is sufficiently capitalized to meet its obligations. After all, if the sponsors as individuals are stockholders in the general-partner corporation, their liability is limited, too. Unless the corporation has sufficient money in it to meet all of the general partner's obligations, it could cause the venture to fail, due to its inability to meet the responsibilities of a general partner. The same is true of the company which manages the property. If it is also a corporation,

the syndicate investors have no recourse to the sponsors personally if something goes awry. This may sound frightening, but the investor must learn to rely to a great extent upon the fact that this prospectus has been registered with the SEC or a state authority. And although such a registration provides no ironclad guarantees, it does prove that an official agency with considerable expertise in such things is satisfied that full disclosure has been made.

8. Needless to say, the prospectus must set forth what yield the syndicate investor can expect from his investment. The full description of the building's tenants combined with the description of the mortgages and taxes should give a clear indication of the property's cash flow and how it will be distributed to the syndicate owners. There will be hedges, to be sure. Even if one buys a building alone, there are risks which do not disappear in a group venture. But a careful study of the cash flow projection should provide a good indication of the return on investment, if all goes according to plan. Also, the prospectus must state clearly how the cash flow is to be distributed and how often. It should state how the profit is to be allocated among the investors in the event the syndicate decides to sell the property for more than it paid for it. If anyone, notably the syndicator, has what is known as an "override" on the building's income or profit on resale, this must be clearly described in the offering statement.

9. Finally, the prospectus should spell out the tax consequences of the investment and its yield. As in singly owned property, income from real estate syndication may be partially exempt from ordinary income taxes. Many investors join syndicates partly because of the tax shelter. (An explanation of how this tax shelter operates appears elsewhere in this book.) Suffice it to say, the astute investor should examine this part of the offering statement carefully, always keeping in mind, however, that the tax opinions offered are just that—opinions of tax lawyers which could vary from the interpretation of the Internal Revenue Service at income tax return time.

It should be obvious, therefore, that a formal prospectus of this type provides the investor with all of the information he needs or could hope to obtain. If, on the other hand, he plans to participate in a small group venture which is not subject to government scrutiny, the prospectus may turn out to be little more than a typewritten outline of what the syndicator proposes to offer the investors. It should be stated that even the government looks upon such small groups as suitable only to substantial and sophisticated participants. In fact, the government specifically requires that the syndicator prove that his investors have sufficient financial capability and know-how to participate safely with large sums in an unregistered real

162 *Real Estate Securities*

estate venture. However, if an investor seeks to join such a small group, he would do well by confronting the sponsor with the questions which arise from an examination of a parallel prospectus which *is* registered. He should have assurances, and preferably in writing, that the property is being purchased, financed, and managed exactly as the syndicator has promised in his brief and informal offering. It is, after all, the only assurance he will ever get before he pays his money.

Investments in real estate syndicates vary in size. There are relatively few left in which the small participant can join by buying units of $5,000. There was a time when syndicators wooed the small participant, but raising one million dollars on this basis was a herculean task of salesmanship, and entailed a registration similar to the one required for issuance of stocks. Today, the trend is to assemble smaller groups of more sophisticated investors by offering participations in denominations of $25,000, though there are exceptions on both the higher and lower side.

JOINING A SYNDICATE

This involves nothing more than the signing of a partnership agreement. And while these contracts are undoubtedly prepared by lawyers, an investor should not forego a consultation with his own lawyer before committing himself. On the other hand, investing in a syndicate relieves the investor of all the responsibility of buying and managing the property. While he normally receives progress reports and financial statements annually or quarterly, he has no voice in the management of the syndicate as a limited partner. In this sense, his position differs little from that of a stockholder in a corporation.

Chapter 15
Real Estate Investment Trusts

One question that came up earlier was: Why form partnerships when there could be corporations? This question occurred to real estate syndicators as early as the 1950s. Their reasoning was logical. For decades, there had been corporations which built or owned real estate, but they did not spring from syndication. However, realty syndicates became popular during the 1950s, and some were more successful than others. A single sponsor could have syndicated seven properties, five of which were doing extremely well, and two that were encountering problems. It gave the investors in those two unsuccessful properties little comfort to know that the same sponsor also operated five flourishing ones.

One way to spread the risk, syndicators found, was to pool the syndicated properties into a single corporation, giving each syndicate partner a stake in all of the buildings by giving him corporate shares in place of the partnership participation. The investor's liability would be limited as a stockholder, and his return would reflect the overall success of the various properties combined. Many groups of syndicates thus converted to corporations in which the various properties, once owned by limited partnership, were pooled.

There was a problem, however. Under tax law, corporations must pay corporate income taxes on their earnings (in this instance the yield on the properties) before they can distribute dividends. This meant that stock-

164 *Real Estate Securities*

holders would be taxed twice—once when the corporation paid its income tax and again when the investor received his dividend. This, of course, diluted the investor's yield considerably. The government came to the rescue, however, with a law which recognized the tax immunity of Real Estate Investment Trusts. In most respects, REITs resemble corporations which own and operate real estate, with one important difference. Under the REIT law, a Real Estate Investment Trust is not subject to corporate income tax provided that it distributes at least 90 percent of its cash flow to investors. Corporations normally do not pay out anywhere near this amount in dividends. The government took the view, however, that the REIT provides an adequate solution to the real estate company which is desirous of paying its income directly to the property owners, or shareholders.

THE REIT

In the REIT, therefore, we have an entity which serves many of the same purposes as does syndication. In addition it enables the investor to spread his risk among many properties and still avoid double taxation. Moreover, in the cases of some REITs, there is an attractive tax shelter. In some ways, it even resembles a mutual fund, all of whose investments are in realty.

Unlike syndications, investment trusts are easy for the investor to find. Many are listed on the stock exchanges or sold over the counter by securities brokers. A good many of them advertise to find investors. All of them are subject to the scrutiny of the SEC and state agencies. Some are even sponsored directly by securities firms or bank holding companies as a financial service. As a consequence, every REIT must make a formal prospectus available to prospective investors and render annual and quarterly reports to the shareholders.

One of the attractive features of the REIT format is the flexibility to invest in various forms of real estate ownership. Just as some mutual funds specialize in certain industries and others hold a general stock portfolio, realty trusts can go either route. For example, there are many REITs which invest solely in mortgages. Then there are those which diversify their holdings among residential and commercial properties, shopping centers, industrial buildings, and mortgages. An investor, therefore, can do pretty much the same things he would accomplish by assembling his own real estate portfolio, except that he does not need to select or operate his properties. Unlike syndicates, real estate trusts do not commit themselves to a regular payout. Rather, they operate more like corporations, which pay dividends when they have profits. Unlike corporations, however, REITs must pay out 90 percent of their cash flow and will raise or lower their dividends to reflect it. Of course, if there are setbacks, they will also skip or discontinue dividends, as has been predominantly the case during the recession of 1974–75.

As in all investments, there are risks in real estate trusts. Properties owned by REITs can fail to produce sufficient income to meet their mort-

Real Estate Investment Trusts **165**

gage obligations or produce a profit for the owner, and REITs may hold the mortgages or own the buildings. Especially during the siege of extremely high interest rates, and recession coupled with rising costs of heating fuel and labor, properties have been unable to pay the interest they owe REITs on the mortgages held by them. As a result, there have been numerous cases in which REITs have had little or no cash flow to distribute. Some have come to the brink of bankruptcy. This, in turn, has depressed the value of REIT shares, affecting not only the trusts whose properties are in trouble, but REITs as a group.

ANNUAL REPORTS

Perhaps the best way to analyze how REITs operate is to take a broad view of their annual reports. In essence, these reports resemble those of industrial corporations. They provide a balance sheet and a statement of income, as well as auxiliary statements showing such items as shareholders' equity, changes in financial position, as well as source and application of funds. They detail their holdings in property and mortgages with photographs, much as do corporate annual reports. Their income statements eventually break down their net earnings per share, and all of them show the net amount paid out in dividends as well as the dividend per share. What becomes readily apparent is the fact that the dividends represent at least 90 percent of their cash flow, as required by law, to exempt REITs from corporate income taxation. Indeed, in good times some trusts pay out more than their net earnings for the year, reflecting the fact that the cash flow, including noncash items such as depreciation, is greater than the income itself. This will be explained later. The recession of 1974–75 has cast a serious pall on REITs. Notably those whose portfolios consisted of mortgages and construction loans have been most seriously affected. Properties beset by rising operating costs have defaulted on mortgage payments owed REITs. Builders who borrowed construction loans from trusts found that they a) could not complete their buildings in view of rising costs for materials and labor and b) saw the demand for the apartments or offices they were building dwindle away in a faltering economy. Some stopped construction midway.

Cut off from their anticipated interest income, many REITs were forced not only to suspend dividends (there were none to distribute) but also to negotiate all kinds of loans to tide them over. Those REITs which owned primarily income-producing properties felt the pinch somewhat less, perhaps no more than any property owner during an economic downturn. Altogether, trusts fell upon hard times as a result of the recession-inflation crunch, their shares dropped sharply in the market, and their investors had to settle for little or no return.

Having said this, it remains for us to look at REITs as operating entities on the assumption that economic recovery will restore them to normal health. To do this, we shall look at the following examples based on their invest-

166 *Real Estate Securities*

ments and performance during a more affluent period prior to the recession:

1. There is one REIT which specialized in all types of mortgages. These included loans on residential and commercial buildings, loans on land held by someone for future development, and short-term construction loans to builders. The total portfolio was about $290 million, yielding an interest income of $27 million. This included about two million in so-called commitment fees, money paid by real estate people to a mortgage lender just for reserving the money until the day when the mortgage would be funded. Of the $27 million, nearly $19 million wound up as net income after operational expenses. With about seven million shares in the hands of investors, this resulted in earnings of $2.70 per share. In this instance, the trust actually paid out the entire $2.70 as dividends. The rate of return depended, of course, upon what each individual investor paid for his stock.

2. Another trust had a total portfolio of about $255 million. The bulk of it consisted of mortgages, but subsequently the trust also began assembling some properties for direct ownership. At the time of one recent year's report, its mortgage holdings totaled about $228 million, and the apartment houses it bought were valued at $25 million. Appropriately, its interest income from the mortgages was about $18 million, reflecting an average interest rate of 7.9 percent. In addition, the trust reaped rental income of $2.5 million from its apartments. Its earnings per share came to $1.04, and it paid out dividends totaling $1.05 per share. How did it manage to pay out more than its net income? The depreciation on the apartment buildings undoubtedly provided the extra cash flow.

3. Let us take a closer look at the makeup of another trust's investments. It had about $97 million in mortgages and an additional $88 million in equities, another term for ownership in properties. This REIT was well diversified, as can be seen from this rundown. Its mortgage loans are broken down in table on page 167.

   This makeup of investments reflects some interesting concepts about real estate. Construction loans, which represent more than half of the mortgage investments, are considered highly profitable (though risky in a recession) in that they command a high rate of return and are intended to be replaced when the buildings are constructed. At that point, the construction loan is normally repaid and replaced with a permanent mortgage. There is little risk in the standby commitments, since they consist of money seldom actually conveyed to the borrower. It is merely money held in abeyance for his needs, and for this he pays a stipulated fee comparable to a low interest rate. Sometimes, of course, the standby funds are called upon for conversion into an actual loan, at which point the proper interest rate comes into play.

Construction loans to builders	**59.7%**
Standing mortgages (mortgages which are not reduced but become payable at maturity)	**9.4%**
Wrap-around mortgages (those in which the second mortgage carries with it responsibility for the first mortgage)	**6.4%**
Mortgages on land held for development	**6.4%**
Standby commitments (i.e., money held ready for the time an owner needs the mortgage, a service for which he pays a fee)	**5.3%**
Long-term first mortgages	**2.5%**
Other short-term loans (probably second mortgages)	**10.3%**

The same trust's portfolio of properties it owned looked like this:

Shopping centers	**38.2%**
Motels	**29.1%**
Office buildings	**26.8%**
Apartments	**2.6%**
Miscellaneous	**3.3%**

The trust's own properties provided a somewhat different balance of risk factors. Shopping centers, depending upon their location and quality, can be safe investments with a good yield if the major tenants (department stores, for example) are financially sound. Most shopping center leases, as was discussed earlier, contain percentage clauses, so that as the retailer's sales volume rises above a stipulated amount, the landlord also shares in the benefit by virtue of increased rent. Motels, on the other hand, are not quite so reliable. Fashions change, and so do travelers' habits. A new motel with more attractive amenities might be built nearby and could cut sharply into the income of the older one. Office buildings can be sound and so can apartment houses, though both are affected by neighborhood changes. Office buildings, however, require longer and more secure leases from financially stable tenants, while apartments are rented on a one- to three-year basis entirely on the basis of the financial dependability of individuals.

4. One particular REIT reported gross income of slightly more than $13 million, with $8.5 million coming from rents in the properties it owned and $4.8 million from interest yielded by its loan portfolio. Against this, the trust had operating expenses of $604,000. In addition, it reported other expenses of $9.7 million, including interest on the mortgages on the properties it owned totaling nearly three million dollars. Another $3.2 million of expenses was depreciation and amortization which, as we learned earlier, are not really money paid out but are considered

168 *Real Estate Securities*

part of the cash flow and therefore must be shown in the financial statement as an expense against income. During the year, the trust also sold some property and realized a gain of more than $400,000. The "bottom line"—the net income of this REIT—came to $3.5 million, which meant $1.06 per share. Of this, 12¢ per share came from the $411,000 netted in the sale of some properties. During that year, the trust distributed more than its net income. It paid out $1.34 per share. This was broken down into return on invested capital of 28¢, ordinary taxable income of 90¢, and capital gains income of 16¢.

This is important to the investor when it comes time for paying his own income taxes. The 28¢ of return of invested capital was not subject to income tax, since it was merely a matter of receiving one's own money back, in theory at least. The 90¢ was ordinary income and therefore fully taxable. The remaining 16¢ was a capital gain and subject to the much lower capital gains tax. An investor who purchased 1,000 shares in this trust, for instance, received $1,340 as his return. However, he paid ordinary income tax on only $900 of it, and a maximum of 25 percent capital gains tax on $160 of it. This again reflects the tax-shelter advantage of investing in real estate.

5. Just as mutual funds have sprung up in the past three decades as a way for the investor to participate in several corporate investments simultaneously, so has the real estate industry developed its own type of mutual fund system. A mutual fund, of course, is a company which invests primarily in the shares of other corporations. Some hold a broad spectrum of stocks, while others specialize in specific industries, growth stocks, or in income securities. It is obvious, therefore, that a mutual fund can also be built around investments in REITs only.

Many more examples of realty trusts could be given, but they follow essentially the same pattern. As a result of the recession, their troubles would also be parallel, with some faring slightly better than others. When they operated profitably—and if they are eventually restored to their previous vigor—their advantages lay in their ability to offset the drawbacks of one property by the success of others, or by compensating for a weakness in mortgages with strength in equities or vice versa. Like all securities investments, REITs are entirely dependent on the skill and foresight of their managements.

Chapter 16
Real Estate Stocks

A final form of real estate investment is stock ownership in companies involved in real estate. In essence, these are not real estate investments as such, but rather the shared ownership in corporate entities which differ little from manufacturing corporations. From the standpoint of the investor, it is largely a matter of holding securities for the long run or trading in them as he would in any stock.

There is a wide variety of such corporations covering a number of different real estate activities. Let us merely list them here, since there are few common denominators.

1. There are several companies which own and operate properties in various parts of the country. Some own office buildings, hotels, motels, shopping centers, or apartment buildings. In some ways they resemble the REITs, but their dividends are fully taxable as ordinary income, save in some instances where the cash flow includes return of capital. Investment in these corporations must rely entirely upon their ability to choose good properties for their portfolio and to operate them profitably. Naturally, they can be hurt by vacancies or economic factors which may depress rents or inflate mortgage interest. This has been the case during the 1974–75 recession.

170 *Real Estate Securities*

2. Construction companies are another category. However, within this field there are several classes, including:

(a) Construction and engineering concerns, which act as general contractors for major construction, such as office buildings, apartment developments, and the like. Their success depends primarily upon their ability to obtain contracts for new buildings. In this group one might also include corporations which serve as subcontractors, providing concrete foundations, steel erection, electricity or plumbing to general contractors. All of these, general and subcontractors alike, are dependent upon the economic climate which fosters new construction (slowed during the recession), though their success or failure also reflects the capabilities of management.

(b) Home builders also have gone "public," meaning that their stock is traded on the market. Some specialize in one-family and possibly two-family developments, while others go in for apartment building, notably the garden-type apartments which resemble one-family housing structurally. What distinguishes these companies from the individual builder whose stock is not for sale is their volume and ability to build in various parts of the country. The typical home builder seldom erects more than twenty houses a year. Corporate builders, on the other hand, count their products in the thousands. And while the individual builder usually operates near his home base, the corporation may have projects under way throughout the United States and sometimes in foreign countries as well. Their income growth should be commensurate with the need for housing, but it is also affected by the mortgage market and the economy in general.

(c) In addition to corporations which engage solely in home building, there are those which have a building subsidiary or division. Some are conglomerates covering a wide variety of industries, home construction being just one of them. Another type is the corporation which entered the home building business from a related field, such as lumber or other building supplies. The reverse is also true at times; construction companies sometimes branch out into fields unrelated to real estate. In these cases, the investor must judge the overall performance of the company and its stock to make a sound judgment on buying its shares.

(d) There are many services needed to keep the real estate industry going: mortgage banking, title insurance, general insurance, building maintenance and cleaning, building supplies, elevators, and many more. These products and services are supplied by companies which specialize in them, and by subsidiaries of diversified corporations. Here, again, the investor must rely upon the general growth and earnings record of each corporation if he considers its stock for investment.

Real Estate Stocks **171**

(e) Since the 1950s, land development corporations have had their ups and downs. These are the companies which sell building lots and larger land parcels in such areas as Florida, Arizona, and New Mexico. As a rule, such companies buy huge undeveloped tracts in a given locale, develop them with roads and utilities, municipal services, and community centers, and offer lots to individual buyers. Some are advertised as retirement communities, while others are entire new towns. The popularity of each area, as well as the general economy, certainly have their effect upon the success of each venture. More important, however, are the accounting principles used by any such company in reporting to its shareholders. Time was when a company of this type could report a sale of an $800 lot the moment a buyer put down the first $10 installment. When that buyer eventually failed to go through with his purchase, this form of accounting would come home to roost and plague the company books with tremendous write-offs. Accounting principles and the laws pertaining to them have since been strengthened by the Securities and Exchange Commission and by many state laws requiring them to report sales to the extent that they have been paid. As a result, these stocks are no longer as volatile as they once were when they rose to enticing heights and then collapsed when the write-offs were taken. The soundness of such securities must also depend upon the quality of the communities which are being developed. Some of them are rapidly burgeoning as healthy municipalities, while others remain arid wastelands. Each investment in such shares must be weighed against all of these factors. In some cases, land development concerns are parts of diversified corporations, and the overall performance of the company, rather than that of its realty subsidiary, must be judged.

To stretch the point, there are many other companies whose shares could be construed to be realty stocks. These include steel, copper, asbestos, gypsum, glass, cement, and many other products which find their way into buildings of all kinds. However, it is not our purpose here to delve into this type of stock investment.

Suffice it to say that there are numerous ways in which the passive investor, not inclined to buy, sell, or operate real estate personally, can participate in the profits of real property.

Index

Accountants, 131–32, 134
Amortization
  defined, 15
  of leaseholds, 15, 106
  of mortgages, 15, 17, 30, 59, 60, 66, 67, 68, 81, 93, 99,
       104, 115, 122, 135, 148, 151, 152, 167
  self-, 24, 68
Appraiser, 118–19, 123
Assessment, 41, 104, 131
  defined, 15, 25
  front foot and, 19
  at percentage of market value, 14–15, 81
Ayer Directory of Publications, N. W., 51

Balloon, 17, 65, 67, 68, 95, 135, 159
  defined, 15
Bankruptcy, 97, 138, 165
Bishop's Reports, 93
Brokers. *See* Realtors
Building codes, 108, 114
  defined, 15

Capital gains
  defined, 15–16
  depreciation and, 17
  taxes on, 15–16, 17–18, 26, 68–69, 81, 82, 122–23, 168

Capitalizing a return, 115
Carrying charges
  on commercial and industrial property, 93, 94–96
  on condominiums, 17
  on cooperatives, 17, 60
  defined, 16
  on farms, 56
  on four-family houses, 45, 47
  on one-family houses, 31, 42
  on stores, 67–68
  on two-family houses, 32
  on vacant land, offsetting, 82
Cash flow, 115–16, 136, 161, 165, 166, 169
  defined, 16, 53, 68, 115
Commercial and industrial property
  leasebacks, 97–100
  net, and net, net leases on, 22, 91, 92–97
Commitment fee, 16
Condominiums, 59
  defined, 16
  maintenance costs for, 58, 59
  vacation, return on investment, 60–61
Constant payments, 25, 115
  on commercial and industrial property, 93, 94–96, 98
  defined, 17
  on four-family houses, 45

Index **173**

on leasehold, 104, 105
on one-family houses, 31
on residential property, 135
on stores, 65
on two-family houses, 32
Construction loans, 165, 166
defined, 17
take-out and, 17, 25, 71
Cooperatives, 59–60
defined, 17
rental and sale restrictions on, 61–62
tax assessment on, 17, 60
Cost base, 16, 17–18
Credit investigations, 93, 138, 140

Deeds, 59, 78, 80, 81, 86
bargain-and-sale, 18, 124
defined, 18
quit-claim, 18
warranty, 18
Depreciation, 16, 56, 116, 165, 166, 167
and capital gains, 17, 68–69
defined, 18
methods of, 123, 133
as tax deductible, 17, 25, 46–47, 53, 54, 68, 95, 96, 107, 123
Down payment, 124, 127
Dun & Bradstreet, Inc., 93

Earnest money, 18, 80
Easements, 76, 78, 125
defined, 18
Engineer's evaluation, 108, 120
Equity, 58, 60, 140, 150
defined, 18
Escalation clause, 19, 70, 160
Escrow, 19, 128
Estates, 39, 40

Farms
carrying charges on, 56
mortgages on, 56
property selection, 55
tenant and crop selection, 55–56
as vacation homes, 55–57
Federal Housing Authority (FHA) loans, 30, 31, 40, 44
Fee
defined, 19
ownership, 101–102, 107, 109–10
Florida Land Sales Commission, 88
Foreclosures, 84, 107, 127, 150–52, 155
defined, 19
Four-family houses
average monthly costs, 44–45
disadvantages of, 46
property selection, 43–44
Front foot, 64–65, 78
defined, 19

Gross rental area, 69, 141
defined, 20, 22
Ground rent, 105, 107, 108, 109
defined, 20

Heat, average costs of
for four-family houses, 45, 46
for leaseholds, 105
for one-family houses, 31, 46
for residential property, 116
for stores, 67, 68
for two-family houses, 32
for vacation homes, 49, 52

Improvements, 141
defined, 20
Income-producing properties
contract for, 124
garden apartments as, 114, 134–35
inspection of, for purchase, 117–18, 120
management of, 128–35
multi-use industrial buildings as, 142
office buildings, 136–42
residential, 111–35
residential vs. commercial, 113–14
return on investments, 114, 116, 135
tenant selection, 140–41
Industrial property. *See* Commercial and industrial property
Installment sales, 86–89
rescission rights, 89
Institutions, 64, 71, 92, 107, 144, 152, 155
defined, 20
Insurance, 30, 36, 160
on commercial and industrial property, 94–96, 98
on condominiums, 59
on cooperatives, 60
on farms, 56
on four-family houses, 45, 46
on one-family houses, 31–32, 46
on residential property, 131
on two-family houses, 32
on vacation homes, 49, 52
Interest, mortgage, 30, 59, 60, 64, 81, 87, 93, 96, 99, 104, 115, 148, 152
as deductible, 33, 36–37, 46, 53, 87
defined, 20
rates, 23, 65, 66, 93, 120, 122, 135, 148, 151, 152, 154–55, 159
Internal Revenue Service, 106, 161

Land
commercial or industrial, 83
development projects, 86–87, 171
extra, with one-family houses, 38–42
as percentage of property's value, 40, 49, 103
in resort areas, 83
retirement communities, 87–89, 171
selecting, 39, 52, 75–77, 82
vacant lots, 75–85

174 Index

Landlord
  defined, 20
  of leaseholds, 20–21, 107, 109
  responsibilities of, 129–34
Lawyers, 119–20, 123, 124, 125, 127, 130, 131, 134, 138, 142, 162
Leasebacks, 97–100
  defined, 20
Leaseholds, 20, 101–10
  amortization of, 15, 106
  defined, 20–21
  ground rent on, 20, 105, 107, 108, 109
  mortgages for, 104–105, 109
  renewal option, 108–109
  return on investment, 105, 106
  term of ninety-nine years, 102, 107
Leases
  commercial and industrial, 92–93, 114, 137, 139, 140–41, 149–50
  escalation clause in, 19, 70, 160
  net, and net, net leases, 22, 91, 92–97
  percentage clause in, 23, 70, 159, 167
  provisions of, 33–36, 70, 137–38
  residential, 114, 130–31
  terms of, 82–83, 137, 139, 159
  for vacation homes, 51
Lessee and lessor, 20, 21, 107
Leverage, 41, 45, 101, 146
  defined, 21, 45–46
  of leasehold, 103, 106
Liens, 126, 128
  defined, 21, 99
  first mortgages as senior, 150, 152
  tax, 21, 25, 79, 84–85
Loans. See Construction loans; interest, mortgage; mortgages; prepayment penalties

Maintenance costs, 28, 29
  capitalizing or expensing, 132–33
  on commercial and industrial property, 94–96, 98, 114, 138
  on condominiums, 58
  on cooperatives, 58, 60
  on farms, 56
  on four-family houses, 45, 46
  on leaseholds, 104
  on one-family houses, 30, 31–32, 46
  on residential property, 114, 116, 132–34, 135
  on stores, 67, 68
  on two-family houses, 32
  on vacation homes, 49, 52
Managers, professional, 110, 128–29, 130, 131, 134, 138
Market value, 14, 79, 84, 108–109, 118, 119
  of condominiums, 62
  defined, 21, 80
Maturity of mortgages, 21–22
Mortgage assignment, 22, 121
Mortgage commitment, 22, 59, 92, 123
Mortgages

amortization of. See Amortization on commercial or industrial property, 92, 94–96, 98
  on condominiums, 16, 59
  on cooperatives, 60
  defined, 22, 126, 147
  on farms, 56
  first, 65, 67, 70, 71, 93, 95, 96, 98, 99, 104, 115, 121, 122, 123, 127, 128, 139, 140
  first, lenders of, 150, 155
  leasehold, 104–105, 109
  lenders, professional, 152–53, 154, 165–66
  maturity of, 21–22
  prepayment of, 21–22, 23, 159
  purchase money, 23–24, 64, 121, 123, 140, 153, 154
  on residential property, 121–22, 123, 124, 126–27, 135
  second, 23, 24, 26, 64, 66, 93, 95, 98, 99, 115, 121, 123, 127, 128, 135, 140, 146–55
  second, purchasing of, as investment, 148–56
  standing, 24–25, 64, 66, 81, 93
  third, 121
  on vacant lots, 80
  on vacation homes, 50
  wrap-around, 26, 122, 152
Mortgage service, 122
Mutual funds, 168

National Association of Realtors, 24, 112
National Real Estate Investor, 159
Net usable area, 22, 69

Office buildings, 136–42
Offices, 63, 69–70
One-family houses
  average monthly costs of, 31
  extra land with, 38–42
  vs. two-family houses, 30–37
Over-ride, 23, 161
Ownership format, 132

Partnerships, 25, 64, 70, 156–57, 158
  limited, 21, 132, 157, 158, 160
Percentage clause, 70, 159, 167
  defined, 23
Prepayment penalties, 21–22, 23, 159
Prospectus, 23, 87, 159–61, 164
Punch list, 127, 128
Purchase money mortgages. See Mortgages, purchase money

Real estate, 24
  selection of, 111–13, 117
Real Estate Investment Trusts (REITs), 132, 163–71
  annual reports of, 165–66
  return on investment, 166–68
Realtors, 33, 50, 51, 53, 72, 78, 79, 80, 112–13, 117, 137, 142, 153, 154
  defined, 24
Refinancing, 24, 42, 96
Replacement costs, 136

Index **175**

Residential property, 111–35
Retirement communities, 87–89, 171
Return on investment
  on four-family houses, 45
  on leasebacks, 99
  on leaseholds, 105, 106
  on net, net leases, 95
  on one-family houses with extra land, 42
  on Real Estate Investment Trusts, 166–68
  on residential property, 115, 116, 135
  on resort condominiums, 60–61
  on resort cooperatives, 61–62
  as second mortgage lender, 148, 153, 154, 155
  on stores, 66, 67, 68
  on vacant lots, 81–82
  on vacation homes, 53–54

Second Mortgages. *See* Mortgages, second
Security and Exchange Commission (SEC), 23, 88, 158,
    159, 161, 164, 171
Security payments, 34, 92, 139
Set-up, 72, 117, 118, 119, 148, 160
  defined, 24
Shopping centers, 76–77, 167
Standing mortgages. *See* Mortgages, standing
Stocks, real estate, 169–71
Stores, 63
  average carrying costs, 65–68
  front foot and, 64–65
  mortgages for, 64, 65–68
  return on investment, 66, 67, 68
Superintendent, 129, 133, 138
Syndication, 70, 156–62
  defined, 25
  over-ride and, 23

Take-out
  construction loans and, 17, 25, 71
  defined, 25
Taxes, 30, 36, 160, 161
  ad valorem, 14, 17
  assessment of. *See* Assessment
  on capital gains, 15–16, 17–18, 26, 68–69, 81, 82,
    122–23, 168
  on condominiums, 59
  on cooperatives, 17
  cost base and, 17–18
  deductibles, 28, 29, 33, 36–37, 41, 46, 47, 68, 86, 87, 96

  on farms, 56
  on four-family houses, 45
  leasebacks and, 98
  leaseholds and, 104, 105, 106
  liens, 21, 25, 84–85
  on net, and net, net leases, 94–96
  on one-family houses, 31
  rates of, 25, 104
  on Real Estate Investment Trusts, 132, 163–64
  on real estate stocks, 169
  on residential property, 116, 131, 132, 135
Tax shelters, 113, 123, 133, 161, 164
  defined, 25–26
  depreciation and, 25, 123
  leasehold as, 106, 107, 109
Title
  clear, 26, 78–79, 124
  clouded or defective, 26, 79
  defined, 26
  search, 26, 59, 78–79, 80, 81, 125–26
Title closing, 19, 78, 80, 124, 126–28, 153
Title company, 78, 81, 125, 126, 127–28
Title insurance policy, 79, 80, 81, 125, 126
Torrens system, 26, 79, 126
Two-family houses
  average monthly costs of, 32
  disadvantages of, 36
  vs. one-family houses, 30–37
  tenant selection, 31, 33

U. S. Department of Agriculture, 55

Vacant lots, 75–85
Vacation homes. *See also* Farms
  average monthly costs, 52–53
  furnishings of, 48, 50, 51
  mortgages on, 50
  objectives in ownership, 48–49
  return on investment, 53–54
  tax deductions on, 48, 51, 52–53
  tenant selection, 50–51
Veterans Administration (VA) loans, 30

Wall Street Journal, 50
Writ of certiorari, 14

Zoning laws, 15, 30, 39, 69, 76, 77–78, 82, 84
  defined, 26